Not My Way

Andrea L. Blair, D.M.H.G.

Copyright ©1996 Andrea L. Blair
All rights reserved.

Available from:
Moments of Grace
P. O. Box 302
Washington Mills, N. Y. 13479
Phone: 315-797-2323

ISBN NO.: 1-883520-23-1
Library of Congress Catalog No.: 96-077098

Jeremiah Press, Inc.
Boca Raton, Florida

Printed in the United States of America

DEDICATION

To my three precious children

Kelly, Tom, David

The delight of my heart.

*I dedicate this book to you; it is my legacy.
Its pages contain the greatest treasure I possess,
my experience of God . . .
his reality, his truth,
his faithfulness, his love.*

*This knowledge is my pearl of great price.
My "wealth"
was not attained through worldly endeavors
or measured by its standards.*

*A gift unequaled in value,
it can never be purchased,
only received.
I offer it to you with all my heart.*

"Our children, too, shall serve him for they shall hear from us about the wonders of the Lord. Generations yet unborn shall hear of all the miracles he did for us. Amen."
Psalm 22, Verses 30, 31.

AUTHOR'S THANKS

With my heart full of love and gratitude, I say "thank you" to
Richard, my children, and friends,
without whose love and support this story
could not have been told.

I also thank two special friends,
Barbara Rozanski and Ann Walseman.

I thank you, Barb, for your incredible
friendship, loyalty, encouragement, and love
and prayerful discerning heart and ears.

I thank you, Ann, for your wisdom, insights, and love . . .
patiently waiting at the computer
until you "hear" my voice as I struggle
to tell my story.

My heart felt gratitude to both of you . . .

My special companions on this journey.

ABOUT THE AUTHOR

Andrea L. Blair, D.M.H.G., is an author and speaker whose autobiography, *Not My Way*, takes the reader on her challenging journey as she struggles to overcome the devastation and heartbreak which cancer has caused in her life. Forced to reevaluate her priorities, Andrea searched for and found answers. Her compelling story of courage and faith is an inspiration and invitation to look beyond the perceptible and to believe the impossible.

Married in 1961, Andrea was a housewife and mother until in 1979, circumstances caused a radical shift in her life. She became actively involved in her church in numerous ministries -- prayer group leader, music ministry leader, praise leader, leader of prayer ministry, inner healing, teacher of "Life in the Spirit" seminars, and an ecumenical concert choir member.

She received certification from the School of Evangelization at the Franciscan University of Steubenville, Ohio. It was then that she began actively evangelizing for two years in upstate New York. Andrea has also participated as a presenter in prayer ministry in retreats for abused women.

Andrea and her husband Richard reside in upstate New York where they participate as volunteers with the Catholic Center of the Good News Foundation, a private foundation for Catholic evangelization. Andrea wrote, developed and presented a program for the Center entitled "The Unopened Gift," designed to bring others into a deeper relationship with Jesus Christ.

Andrea considers her relationship with Jesus and the empowerment of his spirit to be her most valued credential as she seeks to proclaim his marvelous deeds as author and speaker.

CONTENTS

PREFACE Most Rev. Thomas J. Costello, Auxiliary Bishop of Syracuse

FOREWORD Rev. Ralph White, OFMC

INTRODUCTION

One	HAPPY DAYS	1
Two	FROM DARKNESS TO LIGHT	4
Three	WHAT WENT WRONG	10
Four	NOBODY BAKED COOKIES	16
Five	NO EARTHLY GOOD	19
Six	INNER HEALING	23
Seven	HIS VOICE	28
Eight	ACCEPTING LIFE	32
Nine	HAPPY FATHER'S DAY	34
Ten	MUCH AFRAID	39

CONTENTS

Eleven	TOUGH LOVE	43
Twelve	NEW WOMAN	48
Thirteen	GIVE IT ALL TO JESUS	53
Fourteen	AMAZING GRACE	60
Fifteen	BACK ON THE CROSS	67
Sixteen	NOT MY WAY	73
Seventeen	HINDS FEET -- I GOT 'EM!	80
Eighteen	I ATE THE CARROT	85
Nineteen	HAVE FUN!	91
Twenty	CROCODILE DUNDEE	101
Twenty-One	MY PRECIOUS JEWELS	109
Twenty-Two	HOLY LAND	116
Twenty-Three	THE HIGH PLACES	122
"THE REST OF THE STORY" A NOTE FROM THE PUBLISHER		131

PREFACE
by
The Most Reverend Thomas J. Costello
Auxiliary Bishop of Syracuse

Andrea has a story to tell. It is the story of her very real experience of God. Her heart's desire has been to share that story, but a sense of powerlessness and dependency, of fear and poor self-esteem have until now muted her.

An apparently sound marriage, the joy of motherhood three times over, a good life—all are suddenly shattered, first by devastating illness and then by inexplicable separation, ultimate divorce and annulment. It was excruciatingly painful. But in the suffering a new discovery, the actual presence of Jesus.

The instrumentality is a prayer group, women gentle and compassionate, who teach God's goodness and mercy. "I know a lot about God, but I didn't know God." The prayer group did know Him and shared a wondrous awareness of God.

"I was in the presence of God. I knew it. God was there with me, really there, a presence so intense and real, a joy so exquisite and profound."

"God seemed to be calling me to a different, deeper level of relationship, and I was hungry to go." . . . "God was more and more real, more and more accessible." . . . "God really spoke to me." . . . "I know that I was loved." . . . "The Creator of the universe was courting me, wooing me. I was in close communion with Him." The common became uncommon. The natural became supernatural.

Andrea's journey to wholeness tells of an ever deepening intimacy with God, a closeness which not infrequently is manifested in tangible ways. So familiar do they become that Andrea is emboldened to ask God for signs even on the physical level, that she might clearly know when God is asking something of her—signs as prosaic as a single rose, a cluster of grapes, off white sheers found at a garage sale. And God responds!

"Writing this book is like heart surgery," Andrea reveals. "I'm giving those who look a glimpse inside." And inside is conviction: "I am God's child, the Daughter of the Most High God."

"I believe the sharing of my story will encourage others." Andrea is right. Read of how, in their unique relationship, God not only listens to her but hears and really responds and answers!

FOREWORD

When one walks through the 'scary' of their history and invites you to journey with them, they are really opening their hearts and giving you an awesome gift. Andrea does just that in *Not My Way*. She offers us a gift, a gift of herself, a gift of God. We walk with her as she brings to life Matt. 25:21: "His master said to him: 'My good and faithful servant, since you have been faithful in small matters, I will give you great responsibilities. Come. Share your master's joy.'"

In her journey, Andrea demonstrates courage, humanness, trust and growth in her relationship to God and man. A word to describe her attitude toward her own healing must be "tenacious," an attitude which I'm sure overjoyed our Lord as seen by His response.

Not My Way is a story of a personal journey that is both complete and continuing. It is an example of how we can take the hand of God and bring Him into our past, to bless our past, and therefore to bless our present, our future. If we will not let God be present to bless our history, our past can be like an eternal cross to carry. Andrea shows us how to let our Lord bless us, past, present, and future. She brings God alive in the little things and therefore He cannot help but be present in the greater things.

The only reason for us to visit our history is to have our Lord bless it by showing us how He can come alive there . . . and so come alive in our present. By doing this so faithfully, by willingly carrying the pain to the person of healing, Andrea brings Christ alive for us in so many ways.

"Well done, good and faithful daughter!"

Fr. Ralph White, OFMC

INTRODUCTION

It is a glorious sun-soaked day in Vail, Colorado; the majestic mountains are dressed in glistening white. Tiny figures descend the mountains with skill and ease. I'm aware of the discipline and practice, the failures and successes necessary before that ease is achieved. The gondolas lift and transport them to the peaks and set them down for the glorious run to the bottom.

They love the mountain, the exhilaration of conquering it, befriending it, being one with it, relying on it for the joy of their experience. They ski!

I'm told the conquering of disabilities is a price worth paying for the victory achieved. How fitting that here in this magnificent winter wonderland, I am preparing to tell the story of my mountain, the love, respect, and gratitude I have for it, and the price required to climb it.

My mountain appeared to me a jagged unsurmountable task, offering only sure and sudden death, far beyond my strength. Hopeless.

The desire of my heart is to tell my story, a familiar, common story of life, love, happiness, joy, heartbreak, and sorrow. My life became a love story so glorious and profound that it deserves telling. It's really everyone's story, but for me, the common became uncommon, the natural became supernatural ... a truth, an answer, a way so simple, so available, so seemingly unbelievable, so real.

1

HAPPY DAYS

Black letters on a white page fail to inspire feelings and emotions. Words formed by those letters give a sense of clarity and direction. They are the only tools a writer has to convey a story. As the pages in this book unfold, I'll attempt to paint a picture of my life full of color, texture and dimension. My heart and emotions can only be revealed by the words that I choose. My story must come to you from my beginnings for you to better understand my journey. I pray you will allow my life to touch yours and bring you hope

My life began as the only daughter of a middle-aged couple of meager material means, but with a vast wealth of love and wisdom. Mom and Dad were precious, devoted people whose singular goal in life was to be good parents. They were honest and moral, hard working, and unselfish.

During my first five years, we lived with my mother's parents and my adoring Aunt Ethel. Much love and attention centered around me, the first and only granddaughter. Our family was close and caring. Many aunts, uncles, and cousins made our life even richer. We valued the relationships that we shared.

My dad's family was distant and rarely seen because of unresolved differences. I never knew them. When I was five, Dad changed jobs and we relocated about twenty miles away to a small town.

My school years were full. I enjoyed close friendships. I was a cheerleader and involved in extracurricular activities. I loved music and art. I played the violin in the orchestra. I also played the piano and organ and sang in the church choir. I was very involved in church activities and never missed Sunday Mass, unless ill. My parents taught the importance of regular church attendance and prayer. I was strictly disciplined and restricted but given a stable foundation and the love and support of my family and friends.

Each year, when school was out, Mom and I headed for

NOT MY WAY

the lakes where we worked hard at a summer resort. Dad came up on weekends—it was great! We worked together and had lots of fun! Not quite the Waltons, but close!

Our involvement with and concern for each other was very important. It was primary to me to be as my parents dreamed—a good girl—to be honest, kind, well-intentioned, and caring. The love and respect, the desire to be good, and the fear of disappointing them blended like a marble cake and formed me. They were not disappointed. They thought I was nearly perfect and that they had done a good job.

My parents saved their whole lives so I could attend college. Neither of them were formally educated, and, therefore, placed a high value on my education. So after graduation, I attended a state teachers college, desiring to please my parents. I struggled for nearly two years, hating it. I hated even more disappointing them and shattering their dream. Finally, I shared my frustrations with them and with their blessing, left college to pursue a career in cosmetology.

I enjoyed working closely with people and was very happy in my profession. While in beauty school, I met a young man—a handsome, Irish man named Tom. I had *never* felt so captivated. I knew he was for me and I knew I wanted to spend the rest of my life with him. He felt exactly the same.

We knew, although we waited three and a half years, that we were to be married. We were so very much in love. We were always separated either by his college or his time in the Navy. Letters and phone calls sustained us. My life was complete when we were together.

His spontaneous humor and Irish wit delighted and confounded me. My upbringing had been much more serious. Joking was rare, and we usually meant what we said. This sense of playfulness was new and fun!

My family loved Tom and his family loved me. So in 1961, we married—a traditional, Catholic wedding, with all the trimmings. It was glorious, as I had always dreamed.

We then moved two hours away and began our marriage. Our life as a struggling, young couple made us strong and creative. What Tom couldn't make, build, or fix, I could sew or create. My skill in shopping increased and "half off the lowest price" became the law of my land. Treasures abounded. The hunt almost always included a trophy prize! Garage sales were fun and became a great source of entertainment. I became an expert at making or making do. We loved working together. It was amazing to see how much we could do with so little.

Together, we created three beautiful children in four years. We worked very, very hard and loved each other and our children. My greatest ambition was attained—to be wife, mother, and homemaker. There was a lot of joy in my heart—deep gratification in my life. We never really lacked any necessities. The extras made us work even harder and value them more. Most all of our vacations were spent camping in a wonderful used tent-trailer which we customized to fit our needs.

Tom's dream was to have a wife and children who loved him *and* an Irish setter. Although we really couldn't afford one, I saved grocery money for months and placed in his arms a red, frisky, temperamental Shannon. With tears in his eyes, he said, "My life is now complete."

When you're taught by example and not theory, the lessons are well learned. My mother's life was centered around my father and me. Her goals, her successes, and her values taught me that what I had was the most valuable treasure available, that when love and quality are in the home and in the relationships in your lives, you have achieved the ultimate success.

We made a wonderful life for ourselves with enough hardships to make us grow and enough fun to keep us happy. Our "white picket fence and modest little house" existence kept our feet on the ground, our hearts at home, and our faith in heaven.

Our children, one girl and two boys, were healthy, intelligent, and fun-loving. They were involved in all the activities that sparked interest and created balance in young lives: Little League, Pop Warner football, cheerleading, music, braces, proms, camping, Disney World . . . we had it all! We were good parents. We spent a lot of quality time with our children, and we loved them. They were surrounded by loving and involved grandparents and many friends. Love abounded.

"Happy Days" was not just in the "50's." I *loved* my life. I *loved* my children. I *loved* my Tom.

NOT MY WAY

2

FROM DARKNESS TO LIGHT

In 1979, Tom became ill—very, very ill. He tried to work, believing that whatever it was would take care of itself, but he felt awful. He began to lose weight and we knew that we'd better seriously investigate what was wrong. It obviously was not going away. Over a period of many weeks, we visited three different doctors. No one could diagnose him.

The allergist thought perhaps it was an allergy to food and required a detailed record of everything he ate. We eliminated foods that he reacted unfavorably to, until all that was left was spring water, tea, bananas, and pears. He lost a great deal of weight rapidly—over fifty-five pounds. It was hell!

He was tormented by ceaseless itching, high fevers, and chills that robbed us both of sleep. It was unnerving. Finally, the third doctor—an internist—detected an abnormality in his lymph nodes and ordered a biopsy. We were to meet with the doctor a week later to go over the tests. However, in a few days, we received a phone call to go directly to the doctor's office. The news we received there struck terror in our hearts. Tom had cancer and was extremely ill, *so ill* that the doctor wanted to admit him immediately. I passed out in the doctor's office.

Because Tom's father died a few years before, losing his life to cancer, Tom wanted to tell his mother and our children personally before entering the hospital. He questioned whether he'd ever come home.

Fear invaded our lives. Unanswered questions screamed mercilessly at us, eliminating our peace and presenting themselves as enemies awaiting to attack every moment.

"Why?" became the loudest. "Why me? What did I do wrong? I've always been a good man, husband, and father." My husband sat with hands folded, staring at the floor. How do you comfort? What can you say to ease the pain, to reassure, to

NOT MY WAY

give hope, when your own fears are exploding within you? "My Tom, not my Tom! *Please* God . . . not my Tom."

An enormous, silent presence filled our home as we prepared to go to the hospital. Unanswered questions darted back and forth when eyes met. Fear moved in. The power that is held in the hand of news—bad or good—is phenomenal. Lives can crash or soar. How fragile we really are.

When we settled Tom in the hospital and visiting hours forced us to leave, we drove to his mother's home. I was afraid he'd never come home again. I was *so* afraid.

I phoned his sister Pat who lived in Florida with her husband and six children. A few months previously, one of her young sons was seriously burned while playing with matches and gasoline. That accident had caused a major change in Pat. She had become faith-filled and talked about thanking and praising God for *all* experiences. We thought she had gone a little off the deep end and lost her reason because of the strain. Pat answered my desperate call.

"Pat," I sobbed, "Tom is in the hospital with cancer. I'm terrified he's going to die!" Pat's reaction was calming and peaceful—completely the opposite of the sick fear that overwhelmed me.

She said, "Andy, do you believe in God?"

I said, "Of course, Pat, you know I do. I'm Catholic. I go to church. I believe in God."

She said, "Then give Tom to God. For God loves Tom more than you do, and only God knows the outcome."

Because of my desperation, I clung to every word that came from Pat's mouth. She spoke with authority.

"Andy . . . fear is not of God. Trust is. God will show you how to pray. Give Tom to God."

Pat then began to relate incident after incident, wondrous stories about experiencing God's presence. She saw God work miracles in her child's healing. She experienced peace, in spite of the difficulties. Her overwhelming conviction and complete assurance that God would truly take care of Tom soothed my heart. I listened further.

Again . . . "Andy, ask God to show you how to pray. He will," she assured me. "Look for signs. God's love for Tom is perfect. Let go of Tom. Give him to God. Let go, Andy. Trust God. Let go!"

NOT MY WAY

Pat continued to instruct me. "Do not surround yourself with people who will be fearful. Trust is needed. God will show you. *Fear* is not of God. It will cause you undue pain and make it impossible to trust. God will show you."

Once again, she pleaded, "Let go. Look for signs."

I began to really listen and hear what she was telling me. I calmed down a little and was amazed at the profound stories she continued to share. How real God was to her! How incredibly real!

"Put a smile on your face. Your smile will show that you trust a power greater than yourself to carry this burden. Trust is needed, not fear. God will show you," she repeated over and over.

During that phone call, as I look back, an amazing thing happened. My fear subsided and I believed her stories, which gave me hope.

How to let go of Tom was beyond my understanding because he *was* my life, my love. I desperately feared losing him. So how could I let go of him? How does one give up—give to God—what one wants so completely? Is that what it means to trust?

Because I felt more calm and peaceful after the phone call, I was able to tell my children some of the wondrous stories Pat had shared about their cousin. God was going to help us! I had never talked quite like this about God before. I was filled with hope and anticipation.

When we arrived home, it was late and the kids went to bed. I was exhausted. My mind tried to absorb everything.

Fear screamed, "Tom has cancer. Tom is dying. He'll never come home. My children? What will we do? If Tom dies, I'll die. I love him so." Terror gripped my mind.

Another voice, the calming voice of Pat, reminded me, "Don't fear. Trust. Let go. Give Tom to God. God will show you. God will show you . . . "

As the battle raged in my head, the phone rang. It was late. It was Tom.

"Guess what I just did, honey?"

"What, Tom?"

"I found a priest and went to confession and communion."

My heart stopped beating. I was filled from the top of

my head to my toes with a sensation so overwhelming, so profound—an indescribable joy that waved over and through my body. *Tom would live! I knew it!*

The knowledge permeated my mind. When I could speak, I said, "Tom, you're going to live. I *know* it!" And I *did* know it.

If we spoke more, I can't recall because the joy continued to encompass me. I never went to bed that night but sat in my living room experiencing an ecstasy that was indescribable. A presence, that I now know to be Jesus Christ, had revealed himself to me. God had given me my answer. Tom would live!

So many truths presented themselves to me. I was in awe of this experience. I was in the presence of God. I knew it! He was there with me. He was *really* there. He was real!

Tom had not been to confession or Holy Communion since the difficult death of his dad years before. To me, Holy Communion is life, victory over death. I *knew* he would live! This was not a coincidence. This was my sign! I believed!

How do you describe the indescribable? Mere words cannot express the experience I had. When knowledge fills all your senses, you are never the same. You're in a place of awareness that explodes within you, awakening things so extraordinary they're nameless: a presence so intense and real, a joy so exquisite, a peace so profound. All night I sat with this Presence.

At dawn, my fear was gone. The sky, the trees, the birds were more beautiful than I had ever seen them. The day was brand new and wondrous to me. I knew God had visited me. I knew Tom would live.

As I drove to the hospital, I turned on the radio, and I was surprised to hear the rhythmic guitar strumming of country and western music. . . we *never* listened to that station. Confused, I was just about to switch to my regular soft rock station when these exact lyrics penetrated my ears, "Give your worries to Jesus . . . Jesus never fails."

I was so stunned by these words, I almost lost control of the truck. How incredible! How clear the message. It's exactly what I believed. I did not need to know more. I was confident. Tom would live. He, however, had not had the same experience. *Big difference!* And *he* was the one with cancer!

NOT MY WAY

The weeks and months that followed were difficult. What I saw with my eyes and believed with my heart were two different things, contradictory and frightening. To be positive and hopeful and remain confident was one of my first really difficult lessons in faith. To go beyond the natural, to remember what I knew to be true—that Tom would live—sometimes stretched me to the breaking point.

To suffer with one you love, to caretake and encourage, is hard work; to cling to an invisible truth, to believe it's your responsibility to believe, in spite of physical evidence, is nearly impossible. Chemotherapy, suffering, pain, unrelenting itching, frightening procedures, tormenting questions, vague answers . . . little by little, though, we saw improvement. We gained hope, and Tom finally came home. It felt so good.

One evening, we were invited by a friend to attend what was called a charismatic healing mass. Neither of us had ever been to one but were open to the suggestion.

However, Tom's leg and knee were badly swollen and painful from a chemotherapy treatment, providing a credible reason for him to refuse the invitation to go to mass. Our children's plans also interfered with our going, but three phone calls changed everyone's plans so dramatically that Tom questioned, "Do you suppose someone is trying to tell me something? Maybe we'd better go."

I agreed and we attended our first charismatic mass. People sang, praised with arms uplifted, were joyful—not at all dignified for a Catholic mass, we thought. Although we agreed that everyone was sincere and seemed joyful and deeply spiritual, we felt it wasn't for us.

At Communion, we were both anointed and blessed. After a short prayer for healing, we returned to our seats. The mass was simple, solemn, beautiful . . . lengthy.

The next morning, I was preparing breakfast when Tom yelled to me to come to the bedroom. He was standing in his short blue terry cloth robe with an incredulous look on his face.

"Andy, look! Look at my legs," he said in awe. "There is no pain . . . no swelling . . . both legs match!" He was so excited. He extended his arms above his head and said, "Praise the Lord!" as we'd seen at the mass the previous night. Tom had received a visible, believable, undeniable healing. How miraculous! Now we both had experienced God's touch.

NOT MY WAY

Later that day, we went out and bought a usable Bible. Our family Bible was "strictly for show," and we never really read it. Now, we began reading together and praying, sharing another dimension of hope, confidence and faith.

Medical procedures, however, were still difficult and the whole ordeal was horrendous! Eventually, life became somewhat normal. Tom eased back to work gradually and even received a promotion. People were so caring and helpful. Chemotherapy was finally over and Tom was scheduled to meet with his oncologist. I agreed to meet him there, since he was now able to work almost full days. The doctor told Tom that he was pleased with his progress and wanted to schedule a return visit in three months to reevaluate him. As we left the doctor's office, Tom was very quiet. I was thrilled.

He went back to work and I went home and prepared a wonderful celebration dinner. I set the table in the dining room with the good china. I was *so* happy. I even baked a "Congratulations, Honey" cake. To me, it seemed like the ordeal was over and we could finally relax and enjoy our life together once again. I was so grateful to God that I had my Tom back, so thankful that his suffering was almost over. It was a time to celebrate.

3
WHAT WENT WRONG?

Tom did not come home that night until very, very late. He didn't call and I was so worried. I could not imagine what happened. This was not Tom. Perhaps he was celebrating and forgot, but that was hard to believe since he would always let me know if he was going to be late. But he was Irish and it was good news, so I figured he just needed to take some time.

Tom began to change radically. More and more frequently, he would come home late and not call me to let me know. I didn't know what was going on. I figured maybe it was a depression or something from the cancer. Understandable, because he'd been through so much. I was so afraid for his health. I thought he should be resting more. I was so very frightened.

Later and later, he came home... three... four o'clock some mornings. My fear turned to panic as I waited night after night wondering what had caused this change. I tried to reassure myself and the kids that Daddy was going through a depression because of the cancer and that soon, he'd be okay.

He couldn't tell me what was wrong. He didn't know. He shared nothing and became so quiet and sullen most of the time—so unlike him. The smiling, twinkling Irish eyes were dark and bleak and so troubled.

At four o'clock one morning, when he came in, I screamed at him, "Tom, what's wrong? You've been through so much. You're going to drive off the road and kill yourself. Don't you care?" I pleaded.

"No, Andrea, I don't care," he said coldly. "I look at you and see nothing. I don't love you. I don't want to be married to you."

An agonizing pain ripped through my body. Terror gripped my heart. The look on his face and in his eyes scared me to death. I believed him. I don't know how many lifetimes passed before I could breathe. My insides were shattered. The only functioning part of me were my eyes, which poured endless tears.

I sat on the side of our bed until morning, unable to move. I couldn't believe this. It made no sense. It was illogical. Yet something deep inside of me did believe it. I was devastated!

The next morning, I attempted to function as usual. We had to go to one of my son's football games. I went through the motions and sat in the bleachers, staring at the field with tears streaming down my face. My insides were filled with emptiness; the pain—deadening and excruciating. My mind couldn't really grasp what he said, because to me it wasn't truth, and yet, I knew somehow that it was *his* truth.

He said we needed to buy a car for me so that he could leave. So many things came at me so quickly and I was totally unprepared for any of it. How could this be? I felt mortally wounded—like I was bleeding to death. And no one knew...

This was October, one week before our nineteenth wedding anniversary. Little did I know the love-knot bracelet I would receive from him carried his message—"He loved me not!"

I tried to believe it would change—that he didn't really mean it, that it was something said when he was in a very low place. Therefore, I made the decision not to tell my children. Any questions that they asked about his strange behavior, which was most everything at this time, I blamed on the cancer. I reassured them that this was an extremely difficult time for him and that things would change and he would be okay. *I* needed to believe that. I made the decision not to tell my friends, my parents ... anyone.

Night after night, I would question him. I would beg him. I would talk to him when he came in, trying to get an answer, trying to understand what had caused this complete change in him. Now, I was fighting for *my* life.

"Have you felt like this for a long time?" I pleaded, with tears in my eyes.

"No," he'd answer flatly.

So many times he said to me dispassionately, "I don't know what's wrong, but I know I don't love you. And if I don't love you, I can't stay here. I can't stay married to you."

How does love end so quickly? What kills it when

there's no reason for it to die? Over and over, my mind screamed these questions at me and I had no answers. I just prayed and prayed and prayed.

I knew there was no "other" woman—that would have made sense to me—this did not! Was I really worse than *no one*??

Could the cancer and chemotherapy drugs have altered his personality so dramatically?

How could this be?

I thought cancer was bad. Now, *I* was faced with death. The death of my marriage . . . the death of our relationship . . . the death of my happiness . . . and I didn't know what to do. There was no treatment. There was no support group. There were no well wishers. There was only terror, despair and hopelessness.

The pretense that everything was okay took all my energy. I tried to protect my children, my parents, my friends . . . I think maybe even myself . . . from the truth of it. The pain that I carried within my heart never left. People knew something was wrong because Tom's behavior was obviously different. I didn't dare speak to anyone about what was going on, though. I didn't want to hear it with my own ears. It was too awful for me.

At one point, a friend called and invited me to a prayer group, realizing I was having a difficult time. I accepted her invitation and walked into the presence of the most wonderful women that God ever put on the face of this earth. They allowed me to sob every single week, without questioning me. Their love strengthened me. I was learning about God and God's love for me.

With Tom, I was desperate and I was fighting for my life. Anything that I could do to save myself, I did. I begged. I pleaded. I manipulated. I threatened. I tried to convince Tom how dangerous his leaving would be for our children—how emotionally devastating it would be for them. I tried it all!

I tried to lay guilt. I tried to compromise . . . to bargain. The terror of abandonment surpassed my reason and my pride, and I was willing to pay *any* price to get Tom back. I prostituted my dignity, my self worth. The ultimate rejection of myself, by myself and by my husband, was more than I could bear. I didn't want to bear it. I really didn't want to live. The pain was too excruciating. But I also didn't want *not* to live because I had three children whom I loved deeply. I was in hell!

Every night, I would beg and plead with Tom. During the day, I would try to survive until the nighttime came. Each night when he came home, I didn't know if it would be the last time that I would have him with me. It was hideous. It was really hideous. I didn't have the courage or the ability to stop begging. I wanted him so desperately. It had been six months of torture and torment, devastation and despair, since he first told me he wanted to leave.

I remember looking at Tom one night, finally, and the love I had for him overwhelmed me. I saw the desperation in his face and his need to leave. My heart bled. I finally was able to say to him, "I love you so . . . I never knew that I could love you so much. But if you have to leave, go! But I won't tell the children. It's something you have to do. If you have to . . . go!"

Tom held me in his arms and we cried together. It was a horrible experience. We were both in a great deal of pain.

Soon after that, Tom told our three children that he didn't love me anymore and had to leave. I sat, watching numbly, observing this nightmare as it played itself out in front of me. Our children ran crying to him and threw their arms around his neck. They held onto each other. To watch their faces was excruciating. I was devastated. What had I done? How had I failed?

Later that afternoon my sons and I watched incredulously as he emptied our closet, packing his clothes, shoes . . . everything! My daughter sat motionless—staring—alone in our family room. Pain registered all over her beautiful sixteen-year-old face. We cried as he drove away. Twelve-year-old David ran out the door, sobbing as he ran across the fields as fast as he could. I started to run after him, but my son Tommy said, "No, Mom . . . let him go." Tommy's eyes swam with tears as he, in that moment, became the man of the house. He took the responsibility for all of us on his young, fifteen-year-old shoulders. He went into the cellar, came up with a hammer, and said, "Is there anything you need fixed, Mom?"

I felt extremely guilty. It was *my* fault that my husband didn't love me. Nothing I could do or say could prevent this from happening. The three hearts of my children broke with mine. Our home was never the same. Emptiness moved in and remained when Tom left. Although we tried our best, the heart had gone out of all of us.

Tom moved in with his mother and I would occasionally—more than occasionally—call to see if he was okay, if perhaps he had changed his mind which, of course, he hadn't.

When you have invested your entire self in another human being, that other becomes your focus. Your life is centered around him. He becomes your god. When faced with the threat of losing him, you face and fear your own death. When he walks out the door, you go with him. Death occurs. The shell that is left is empty, yet full of pain. You walk and you talk and function mostly. You feel that you could shatter into a million, irreparable fragments, like Humpty Dumpty ... never to be put back together again.

The image in the mirror lies to you, reflecting a person. You don't feel like one. The ache within you seems so much larger than you. How can you carry all that weight? Why doesn't it show? Yet, you go on. Your broken heart still carries immeasurable love for him. You hurt for him and for your wonderful, precious children. There is just so much pain.

How can this be? Every hour you're faced with failure. Some unknown flaw that convinces you that you're responsible, that you've caused this circumstance. The " if only's " hammer away at your brain as you search for answers and for a solution, a way out of the pain. You see more failure as you begin to believe that you even fall short in mothering because you can't ease the suffering of your children. More guilt and pain bears down. The questions go unanswered, the pain persists. *If only* he'd come home.

Even your morals trap you. They prevent you from easing the pain yourself. There is no way out of it. You're in it. It's part of you. You need help. Where do you go?

I went to the prayer group and told them the truth. Tom was gone; I was suffering despair, hopelessness; I needed them.

Gentle and compassionate, they let me cry. They understood, and I felt no judgment or blame. They were loving women who studied the Bible. They sounded like my sister-in-law, Pat. They knew Jesus, too. I needed to become one of them. These women taught me about God. They studied about Jesus and his Holy Spirit, about how God loves us and is concerned about our peace and well-being, and how he desires to be personally involved in our lives.

I knew all of that. I had met God in my living room. I knew he had healed Tom, and I knew it was a miracle. And I was so grateful.

In my pain, though, I'd lost sight of God. I hadn't turned to God to ask for a miraculous healing for my marriage as I had for Tom's cancer! The intensity of this tragedy caused me to forget him, but the prayer group reminded me of God's goodness and mercy once again.

A new belief entered my mind and heart and consumed me: A God who healed a man from cancer and returned him home to his family certainly could heal my marriage!

"Please, God, please, bring Tom home."

4
NOBODY BAKED COOKIES!

Now, everyone knew—my parents, our families and friends. I could no longer protect any of us from the truth. Tom was gone. Disbelief, incredulous looks of amazement surfaced when people were told. "Not you two, it's not possible! What happened? You had the best marriage. You've been through so much."

Tom and I always shared so many things and did things together. People could see that we were genuinely happy because we were! It was almost as difficult for them to believe this strange occurrence as it was for us.

We were married almost nineteen years, and the friendships that we had made over this period of time living in one neighborhood were shared by both of us. Loyalties and confusion pitted against each other. "Who should remain friends with whom?" "What do I say?" our friends asked. So many questions!

It's so difficult when a marriage fails and people separate, entirely different than when a death occurs. With a death, neighbors and friends rally around. They support you, care about your well being, take you to dinner. People bake cookies, bring food, sit with you, mourn with you. They send flowers, sympathy cards. They become so involved with your pain and try to help you carry the pain. And that's all exactly as it should be, because it's so traumatic to lose a loved one.

But when somebody walks out the door . . . *nobody* bakes cookies. Nobody really knows what to say . . . not to you, not to your children. You begin to fear that your neighbors and friends wonder, *"What really happened?"* You become paranoid, wondering if you're viewed just a little bit differently now, more harshly. Your own confusion, questions, and guilt condemn you, not your friends. It's just so awful. There's no one who can share the pain of your rejection.

A separation of spouses by death is tragic but normal;

it's in order. Untimely, perhaps, but not a choice. Being rejected is a deliberate choice, a choice made by someone else, not a mutual decision. Rejection convinces you that there's something very wrong with you, that the person who no longer wants to be in relationship with you has discovered something undesirable, totally unlovable. Your desires are of absolutely no consequence. You and your wishes simply don't matter. You and your hopes and dreams are not validated as being worth anything. You have no choice in the matter! You feel powerless. You *are* powerless! You feel like a victim without any rights. In essence, that's exactly who you are! It's hell!

You find that you are now single and the friends that you've had for nineteen years are couples. You feel clumsy and awkward, so self conscious, with them. You don't fit in anymore. Your heart hurts even more watching the intimate glances that pass between husbands and wives, rubbing salt in your wounds. The intimacy, the oneness, the simple act of being in the same house with a couple is so painful when you've lost your partner. You feel like a third wheel, like you don't belong. You feel like a charity case, even though you're not treated that way. Your self worth and dignity vanish. You don't know where to go. You don't know what to do. You so desperately need your friends and you want people around you, but the people around you seem to remind you even more of what you've lost. It's not fair. It's hard. It's very, very hard!

There are stages of grieving to go through when a death occurs; death offers final closure. A natural progression of anger, denial, pain, loneliness and depression occur, but eventually most people get to the point of acceptance. Their loved one has died and he or she will never see them again, at least not in this lifetime. But when somebody walks out the door for no apparent reason and there's a lot of hope that they'll return, you find yourself in a state of limbo, a "nowhere place." You're married but you're not married. You're alone but you're not divorced. You're single but you're not single. You're alone; you're alone!

Nothing works . . . nothing fits. People ask if you're married. Of course you are, but you don't have a husband. People ask if you're single, and you're not . . . but you are! It's awful!

Financially, that's another whole story. Initially, everything seems okay. You believe your spouse will take care of you. When he's no longer in the house, though, he becomes less and less responsible—unaware of what's going on most of the time, forgetting all of the hundreds of little incidences and responsibilities required of parents. You ache as you watch your children suffer.

In a natural death, the children are usually provided for—if not by life insurance, by government assistance. A necessity is acknowledged. But, when you're still legally married, the government takes into consideration the income of both parents as a couple. When you're *not* legally separated, you are at the mercy of your spouse. You might receive a very small portion of that income, but you are responsible for the house, the children, and everything that goes along with raising them. On paper it looks like you have enough to live on. In reality, you don't!

Circumstances attempt to force you into making decisions that you wouldn't want to make. Financially, it's better to be divorced because, legally, you could get support and financial aid. But if you don't believe in divorce and believe that your marriage is going to be healed, you're in trouble! If you don't have enough to live on and won't compromise your beliefs, you find yourself in a pretty difficult situation.

That's what my decision was like.

I believed with all my heart that Tom would come home and return to being the wonderful father, the good husband, the "twinkling-eyed Irishman" that I loved so very much.

He wanted a divorce, and I didn't! The kids were hurt, angry, and confused. "How could you want him back, Mom, if he doesn't want us?" they asked.

I made the decision to wait it out . . . to accept the difficulties and not compromise my beliefs. People tried to convince me that I was making a mistake . . . that I should sign legal separation papers . . . that it would make it easier for us financially and emotionally. But I knew my signature would be admitting that I was willing to be divorced. I was not. I could not sign the papers.

I needed help and there was only one place to go . . . to God. I believed that if I became the very, *very* best Christian lady, involving myself in all things pleasing to God and learning about him and his will, my prayers would be answered—So I did. God offered a tray of cookies and I was hungry.

5

NO EARTHLY GOOD

All my life, I'd gone to church. I had been taught to revere God, to be good, to obey the Ten Commandments. I knew about miracles and believed in God's power and his majesty. I was raised a Roman Catholic and I believed in the Eucharist. I listened to the Gospels every Sunday, as well as the Old and New Testament readings. I knew about tradition in the church. I knew a lot *about* God, although I didn't *know* him.

Since God had initiated this relationship, I decided that I'd better pursue it. I needed to know him. I went back to the prayer group . . . they *knew* him! Amazingly, I learned that a personal relationship with God is what he offered me. How had I missed it? Beats me, but I did.

I knew a lot about God. I also knew a lot about President John F. Kennedy, but it would have taken a personal relationship to barge into the Oval Office and sit on his lap like his little boy (John-John), asking his father for whatever he wanted or needed.

I've been taught to call God, "Father." I could relate to God as Father because my earthly father was good, kind—somewhat intimidating at times—but he loved me and wanted what was best for me. Dad had always taken good care of me, but to understand and really believe that God Almighty was my Father took some doing. I needed to know I was God's child, and on one level of awareness I could grasp this concept. But, *really* . . . my Father? If this was really true, my relationship with God would change drastically. Could I then barge into his heavenly office and climb on his lap?

When you meet someone and really get to know him, fear or intimidation or whatever misconceptions you may have change. Fear diminishes as the relationship grows, and even the names change as intimacy increases. If God is vague, unidentified, and unnamed, he's vague, unidentified, and unnamed. If he is recognized, identified and named "Father," "Abba,"

NOT MY WAY

(Daddy), then my name is "Child." To believe that God was my father, my daddy, and to act like it was quite a new concept for me. I really didn't feel like much of anyone, least of all God's child. My identity, my *major* identity as "Tom's wife" was being destroyed, and I was scared to death. I felt worthless and unlovable.

My prayer group was leading me into deeper understanding of this strange idea of a personal relationship with God and I had much to learn. I had always prayed and hoped that God had listened. I was learning now that God does so much more than just listen. He hears, he responds, and he answers. He says, "Ask and you shall receive, seek and ye shall find, knock and it shall be opened." I soon learned to pray about each new crisis that presented itself—asking, seeking, knocking—crying to God for help in *every* crisis. He gave me so many opportunities to pray!

I had not worked outside of our home since our marriage, with the exception of styling hair for a few neighbors and friends. Homemaking was my chosen and fulfilling career. Even though times had never been financially easy for us, now, with Tom gone and the money he provided becoming less and less, I needed to find work to support us. He was insisting that I take on some responsibility financially. He'd been gone about six months . . .

I had no idea where to begin. I was afraid of everything! Who would hire me? I was forty years old; my last experience in job-hunting was twenty years ago; my resume was pathetic. Also, I didn't want my children to have to return from school to an empty house or limit their extracurricular activities due to no available transportation. The separation was difficult enough for them; I couldn't ask more.

Overwhelmed, I tearfully sat down and began to pray, pleading my seemingly hopeless case before God, when the phone rang. A friend, whose hair I occasionally styled, was a nurse in a nearby nursing home. She called with an emergency: The beautician at the nursing home was no longer able to work full time. They desperately needed someone.

"Andrea, do you think you could possibly help them out? I'm sorry it's such short notice," she said breathlessly, "but I've already told them about you and I think you would be perfect."

NOT MY WAY

I shook my head as she spoke, hardly believing my ears. My heart began to pound.

"Would you please consider it?" she continued. "Even if just for a short time; they're really desperate. Can I set up an interview for you tomorrow?"

As tears rolled down my face, I explained to her that I had not even finished my prayer and it was already answered by her call.

"Thank you," I said. "Yes. Please... set up the interview."

The next day, I gathered up all my courage, put on my "smile mask," and an appropriate outfit. With my heart thudding inside my chest, I walked into the nursing home where I was greeted by the director with appreciation and gratitude. We toured the home and I was introduced to its residents.

"This is your new beautician, if she'll take the job," she said happily to the elderly women we met on our tour. Some of the women—those who *could* —responded with a smile. Others stared blankly up at me, one more nameless face to try to remember.

How perfect! A nursing home! What an appropriate place for God to send me! *I* needed a place to try to recover. I didn't know God was in the job placement business! My hours were flexible, so I could be home when my kids left in the morning and return before they came home from school. Hallelujah! It could not have been a more perfect place for me. Once again, I was reminded that whatever my need, God would fulfill it.

I began work the next day. I'd wheel my customers into the small beauty shop which contained a sink, a desk, and four dryers. Much of my time spent alone with them was in silence, for unlike most beauty shops, my customers were too ill to be laughing and chatting a lot. Talking tired many of them and sitting for long periods to have their hair done was painful to some.

Some of the women became quite angry: I was spit at, bitten, hit with a cane. Curlers were pulled out when I'd turn my back. I had to clean up an occasional puddle on the floor or hold the head of someone who was too sick to retain their breakfast or lunch. I held hands and wiped noses and tears. I cried with them, relating to their hurt and pain. Sometimes, I didn't know for whom the tears flowed, them or me. This job was certainly heaven-sent for me.

Every time I'd pray about something, I'd wait for God's answer to me. When I recognized his response, my heart would pound as a thought or sudden insight would enter my mind and be repeated over and over until I understood it.

My situation became clearer as I slowly realized that this relationship with God as my father required an additional response from me. Since I believed it was only a matter of time until the effects of Tom's ordeal with cancer and chemotherapy would change and he would come home, I could use this time to become better.

When you've given all you had to give and you're not wanted—you're rejected—you believe that you're no earthly good. I went above this earth for love and acceptance and I found it.

6

INNER HEALING

I was becoming more and more comfortable and familiar with this wondrous awareness of God, more able to read and understand Scripture, better equipped to pray, asking God to fill my needs.

I was faithfully attending my Wednesday morning prayer group and so was grateful for its holy women, who had become my special friends. On one occasion, we prayed for a spiritual director—someone to help us discern God's will in our lives and for our parish. We believed that a priest would be appropriate.

The following Sunday I went to mass, and during the celebration, our new associate pastor was introduced for the first time. This kind-looking priest began to speak . . . *slowly* . . . "My . . . name . . . is . . . Father . . . Regis . . . Rodda . . . . R-e-g-i-s . . . R-o-d-d-a." I could see the people around me glance sideways at each other and shift uncomfortably in their seats. I heard no audible groans but perceived some silent ones.

But, my heart began to pound. The thrill I'd experienced once before began again—chills, a presence, an awareness. This feeling was God. I recognized it. The joy that flooded me was intense.

Who was this priest?
Why was I feeling this?
Was God telling me something?

My heart continued to pound through mass while tears filled my eyes. The joy that I felt showed as I waited my turn to speak to him after mass, welcoming him to our parish. I invited him to attend the prayer group with me and he smiled, nodding acceptance. I knew God had provided once again. I drove to the home of a couple whose friendship and love I shared and told them of my experience. They, too, had recognized God's gift and were thrilled.

Father Regis was our answer to prayer. He accepted our invitation and filled the position of spiritual advisor. He brought to our prayer group knowledge and profound spiritual gifts. We all learned as he influenced us toward a clearer, more well-defined understanding of relationship with God. Now, with his prayer and spiritual direction and the love and prayers of these holy women, my pain and life were being healed. God was becoming more and more real—more and more accessible. I was learning a lot—reading and studying and praying. My desire to be all I could be for God was similar to my desire to please my earthly father.

My friendship with Fr. Regis was clearly a special gift from God. His knowledge and giftedness in prayer helped increase my knowledge of God and I wanted more. He became my spiritual director.

God seemed to be calling me to a deeper level of relationship and I was eager to follow. When Father Regis suggested inner healing to me, I needed an explanation. My understanding of healing was limited. I knew only of physical healing.

Father Regis explained that from our conception and throughout each moment of our lives we experience different degrees of imperfections in our relationships. This "living" forms and molds us into who we are. Some events are clearly recognized as traumatic and harmful to our healthy development. They can be influenced and changed by prayer. Inviting Jesus into our lives can open the door to healing our deepest psychological scars and restore us to healthier living.

Inner healing is sometimes referred to as the peeling of an onion. Jesus does not cut into our beings exposing our deepest wounds but ever so gently begins at our outer layer with his loving touch and, as if peeling an onion, carefully removes layer upon layer, bringing us closer and closer to our center tenderly touching and healing. Tears of course are present as we shed our coverings and really begin to "see" what needs to be changed in our behavior.

Father continued to teach me about inner healing. "We are sometimes really blind to our own sins and continue in them unaware. When Jesus exposes them we have the choice to remain in them or with his grace try to overcome them."

He smiled as he continued, "Forgiveness is the most powerful tool we can use to restore ourselves to healing. To withhold forgiveness really keeps us stuck and hurts us far more than the one who needs our forgiveness. Sometimes small things grow to enormous proportions and influence bitterness and resentment. This attitude can fester in us and affect us physically as well as psychologically. Jesus wants to set us free from all that holds us bound and heal us. When we say yes to inner healing we willingly allow God to show us what needs his touch. It is a vulnerable place to be because we really are unaware of what God may choose to reveal to us and heal."

Fr. Regis continued his explanation to me. "Andrea, we all experience imperfections, disappointments, and hurts which influence our lives and our responses to life, and we are often unaware of the root cause of these responses and attitudes. Because God has always been with us he knows exactly what's needed. Jesus' presence heals the attitudes and puts them in right order."

"Oh, Fr. Regis," I responded. "How wonderful. I really desire to know what is keeping me bound. How incredible to know that I can be healed of influences from early childhood. Please, I do desire inner healing prayer."

We scheduled a time for prayer and went into the small chapel to begin. We thanked and praised God, expressing my desire to know Jesus more personally. I knew he was real and I knew he had involved himself in my life by healing Tom's cancer. I knew he had heard and answered my prayer and I trusted him.

Fr. Regis prayed, "Jesus, be with us now. Walk with Andrea through her childhood and reveal a memory, an incident, an occasion that you would like to touch and heal." I felt secure and peaceful, welcoming Jesus' calming and gentle presence.

As Fr. Regis prayed, my memory became sharp and clear. Suddenly, I was remembering the house that I lived in as a child, and I could *see* the kitchen and *hear* the sounds of my parents. I could see myself as a little girl of four or five years old. I saw the little dress that I was wearing, and I was amazed that I remembered it. Not only could I see myself, but I could *feel* my emotions: I was upset and angry and feeling hurt and misunderstood. I was frustrated, but I was too young to identify my feelings. And I wanted to run away.

My parents were smiling at each other and I didn't want them to smile. "It's mean to smile when my little heart hurts so," I thought. In a tantrum of wanting sympathy and understanding, I threatened to run away.

"Bye," they said. "Be careful," as they smiled knowingly at one another.

I remembered so vividly walking to the door and turning the handle, looking back over my shoulder and hoping they'd say, "Please don't go, sweetheart." They just smiled and waved, and my despair was complete.

I walked down our back stairs dreading every step that brought me closer to my threatened departure. "Maybe they'll stop me when I reach the yard," I hoped. But they didn't.

We lived two houses from the corner, and although I now know they watched from the upstairs porch, I didn't know it then. I was both stubborn and afraid. My little heart was pounding in my ears and my tummy felt sick. Scary feelings for a little girl. Emotions bigger than me!

I reached the corner and was devastated. I felt trapped since I wasn't allowed to cross the street but couldn't turn around and go back either, feeling so terrible. I stood on the corner crying, feeling rejection which I didn't understand.

I felt just awful as I related this memory to Fr. Regis, who asked me to calm myself. I felt so sorry for her—for me.

He began to speak to me as if I were still that little girl of five, because in reality I was. "Look at the nice man who is coming toward you, Andrea. His name is Jesus and he is very kind and gentle. It's okay for you to speak to him."

I watched as Jesus approached and bent down kneeling on one knee. He looked into my eyes, drying my tears, and smiled. His face was so kind, so sweet and loving. Somehow, even at five, I knew he understood my feelings. Unhurried and patient, he directed his total attention to me, and it seemed like he didn't have anything else to do but to help me.

"What's your name and why were you crying?" he asked sympathetically.

Through tears and sobs, I told him my sad story. "My mommy and daddy don't want me anymore," I whispered. "They let me run away!"

He listened intently. "Your mommy and daddy love you very much, Andrea, but sometimes people aren't always able to understand our feelings and show their love the way we need it." His eyes were soft and loving, and I believed him.

"May I hold your hand," he asked, "while we walk home together? Would you like that?"

NOT MY WAY

"Oh, yes," I said, looking up into his kind and loving face.

He stood up, smiling, putting his strong, gentle hand in mine. Smiling down at me, we began to walk toward my house. "Your mom and dad must be very special people to have such a wonderful little girl! They must be very worried about you and will be so very happy to have you come home."

We retraced the steps I'd taken earlier and knocked at the back door. Daddy opened it, very happy to see me, and I ran into Mommy's waiting arms. "This is my friend Jesus who helped me come home," I proudly introduced him.

"We are so very happy to meet you," Daddy said, "and so happy that you brought our little girl back home to us."

"Andrea," Mommy said to me, "we watched you every second as you walked to the corner. We never wanted you to run away, and we were smiling only because you were so spunky. We didn't realize how your little mind and heart misunderstood our smiling."

We hugged and kissed and laughed, so grateful to Jesus for bringing me home and for healing that upsetting memory. What had seemed a time of rejection, misunderstanding and fear became a time of celebration and healing. Jesus transformed a frightening, confusing emotional experience of rejection and misunderstanding into a special time to meet and know him and to bring him to my parents in love and forgiveness.

How vivid this experience of inner healing was to me when Fr. Regis finished his prayer! We marveled at the restorative power in Jesus, who being the same yesterday, today, and forever, could go back in time with prayer and heal memories that lay dormant, confusing and distorting, robbing us of freedom and holding us in bondage. Retracing the steps with Jesus untied the knot that kept me bound.

God says in Scripture, "I have come to give you life to the full. I have come to set the captives free!" I understood—I wanted this freedom. Heal me, Jesus!

7
HIS VOICE

I went home feeling wonderful. After experiencing inner healing prayer, my understanding was deeper. I *knew* that I *knew* that I *knew* . . . I was loved! I had no doubt that Jesus had been with me since I was a little girl.

I was different. I was secure.

It was late and I wanted to go to bed. Never had I experienced such a feeling of complete acceptance and unconditional love. I climbed into bed, telling Jesus that I *knew* that I was loved. I didn't even have to pray! I felt so secure in his love! I felt a freedom I never experienced before. It was incredible! I closed my eyes and hugged my pillow and was filled with joy.

"Thank You. Thank You. Thank You, God," I whispered.

"*My child*," I heard. "*My precious child.*"

"Who spoke?" No one was there . . . I held my breath and listened.

"*My daughter. My precious. My child*," the words came again. It had to be God. I didn't talk to myself like that. I was awe struck. This is the first time I'd heard actual words. I jumped out of bed, grabbing a piece of paper and pencil.

He continued,

"*I have called you to be mine. I will show you things far greater than the splendor of the mountains, the whispers of the trees, the dancing of the raindrops, the fragrance of my love. My daughter, my precious, my child. Tom will die to self, my way, my time. Rejoice! My will be done.*

Tell my people, "*Love one another. Do my work.*" *Empty yourself so that I may fill you with my Holy Spirit.*"

His presence was profound. I could hardly take it in. I was filled with joy as I sat in my bed, hardly believing what I had experienced. I reread what I had written down. God had *really* spoken to me. God Almighty had said *real* words to me. Of course, I was no longer tired and sat there talking to him, asking him to bless my children, my parents, my friends, everyone I ever knew. I prayed for hours and hours, finally falling asleep.

When I awoke the next morning, I reread what I'd written down and I still couldn't believe it. I dressed quickly and went, as usual, to morning mass. As soon as it was over, I ran back to the sacristy, clutching the paper in my hand that held God's words. Fr. Regis and I both wept as I read them to him. We thanked and praised God, marveling at his generosity.

Thus began a very special time for me. I kept a daily journal and wrote letters to God. "My dearest Lord," "Dear Jesus," "Dear God," I would write and then pour out my heart to him. I told him my needs, my fears, my hopes, my questions and concerns. I'd wait for his response and so often, I would clearly hear his voice and then write down his responses. Sometimes my heart would pound and deep within me, I'd feel a stirring, a stretching, a movement . . . I knew it was him!

Oftentimes, I'd wait, experiencing profound peace, knowing he'd heard. In time, I understood the expression "Living Word" in reference to Scripture, for his words came alive to me. I would hear a Scripture reference in my mind (like "John 10:10" or "Mark 3:7") and look it up, believing that he directed me to it. And he did.

He says in Scripture, "My sheep know my voice." I do know his voice. I know *him*! In understanding and responding to this great love, I passionately desired to know him even more.

"My dearest Lord, " I prayed. "Let me see you. What do you look like? I love you. I desire to look upon your face. Please, my Lord, let me see your face."

He spoke. I wrote,

"My face, my child, is the face of love. It is a blending of every face, of every man, woman, and child that you have ever looked upon.

My face encompasses the wisdom reflected on the face of a rugged, aging fisherman whose skin shows the wearing of time, whose expression acknowledges the greatness of his companion, the sea, at whose mercy he places himself in order to fulfill his destiny.

My face expresses hope. A hope that fills the eyes of a

mother as she looks upon her child and dreams precious dreams for him.

My face lights with recognition of a beloved friend not seen for a time, but met unexpectedly.

My face is patience . . . that of a grandmother whose rocking chair has quieted as she rests her head against its back and accepts her stillness.

My face knows pain . . . lines of truth etched upon a smooth surface giving it depth and quality.

My face is the innocence of a new born child sleeping peacefully on its back in total and complete trust that its needs will be met and satisfied.

My face is that of the expectancy of a bridegroom as he awaits his beloved, his choice for lifetime commitment to share his entire self.

My face, my child, is the face of mankind, my divinity expressed in the individuality of each face, unique in my molding of it. Each face represents a heart, beating in call to me . . life given by me . . . called into being by me . . . allowed to continue struggling by me . . . created for perfection, for peace . . . for joy, created in my image.

Sin has marred that perfection . . . Look about you, my child . . . see me!! Love me!! Love is the answer, the key to unlock frozen hearts—the answer to every need if only you would love one another.

My child . . . drop the veils . . .the chains . . .the trappings . . .the coverings! Step out as they fall about you. Expose your real self to me, for I know you already . . . look at that self with me at your side.

Love that self, for I love you!!
Freedom is yours.
Peace is yours.
Joy is yours.
Life, I give you.

Months afterward, I received a birthday card from a dear and precious man who had become a treasured friend. In the card was a photograph. Someone had taken a picture of unusual clouds and when it was developed, they saw, not clouds, but Jesus' face.

"I do see you, Lord, I do . . . I see your face."

NOT MY WAY

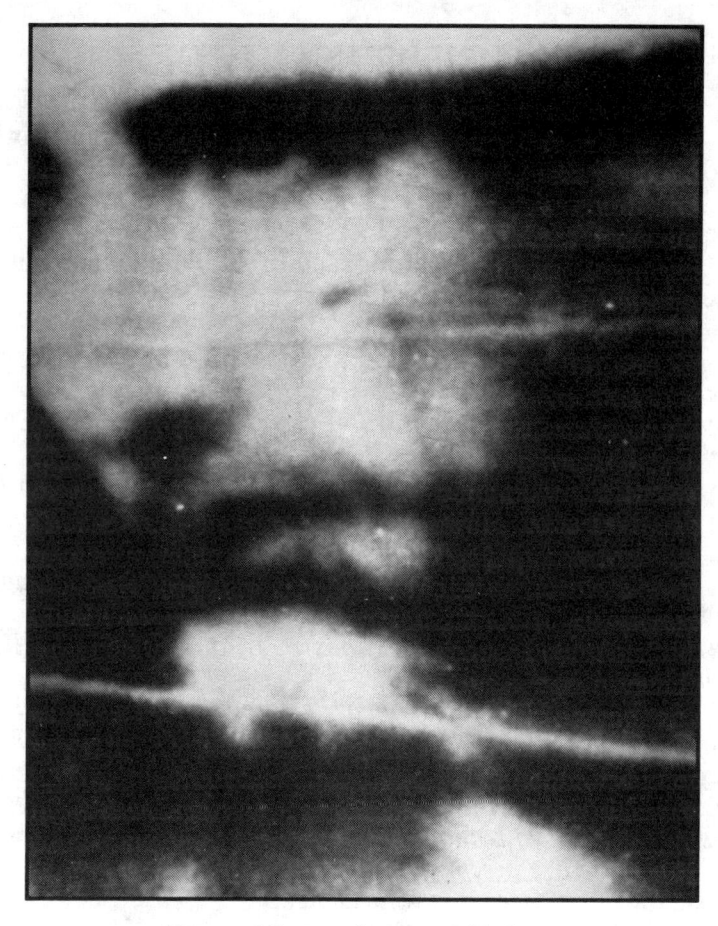

Face of Jesus photographed
in the clouds

8

ACCEPTING LIFE

One night, during a healing mass, I saw a mother bringing her small child to the altar for prayer.

"Why, God, Why?" I questioned. "Why would this little child have such a terrible illness?"

His presence was strong, and I felt I could reach out and touch him. He answered and I wrote,

"My child, you see around you pain of every description. Every manifestation of sin. Every form of corruption. Every mutilation and violation. Every thing imperfect. Everyone imperfect.

Can you not see why? You claim to know me, to love me, to want to serve me, to want to be worthy of the inheritance that I offer. Yet, you still do not understand.

I reveal myself, my reasons, my nature in every page of my Holy Scripture. It was for that reason that I presented it to you. I answer all your questions in it, but you do not listen . . .you do not hear.

When you attempt to hear, you fear the answer and turn your back on me. I desire faces lifted to me in adoration and prayer. I see backs turned from me, shutting me out; rejecting the very source of life, the proper nourishment, the healthy food. Instead, you choose darkness, corruption, evil ways. The turning from me, my children, is ignorance. There is no excuse for ignorance; it is your choice.

I tell you to know, love, and serve me. How, my little ones, can you know me when you will not take time to know me? How can you love me, when you do not know me? And how can you serve me when you do not listen to what I ask?

I place at your feet, within your reach, my very self. I've made myself known to you in Scripture, in the touch of loving friends. I've healed your sick. I've performed countless acts of love and mercy. But you still do not see.

My children, I tell you, set aside time for me, time to

NOT MY WAY

touch me with your eyes, your hearts, and your ears. I will not fail you. I am always with you, you are rarely with me. Listen to my call; learn of me. Be with me. I stand at the door and knock. How long must I stand there? How loud must I knock?

You ask why I allow pain and suffering. It is allowed simply to bring you to the Father —I showed you the way. I lived and worked. I knew joy and sadness, health and suffering. I shared in all things with you and now I offer you all things. If you do not question the good, why do you question the bad? Accept my will for you as your Calvary, your death and resurrection. Know that will by knowing me. In that knowing, trust. In that trust, joy! It is my joy to give life eternal. Accept it in joy!

I understood better the effects of sin and separation from God which originated with Adam and Eve's disobedience. The question and curiosity which is good and in order in man ... can be man's downfall when he goes beyond the natural limits set for his protection and forces knowledge. Man's quest to "know" can bear bitter fruit which poisons the soul.

Lucifer deemed himself to be equal with God. By demanding his right to exercise his own will, he placed his designated and lofty position in jeopardy and fell. In whatever way he can, he continues to trick and deceive, raging against God and God's children, causing us to fall further and further from God ... deeper and deeper into the hell of lies and distortion until the peace and love and beauty of God's paradise becomes uncommon and unnatural to us. Lost.

The truth is that we were created without sickness and disease, without malice and hatred, in continuous fellowship with God our Father. We can undo what's been done by determining in our own will to do God's will. We can live resurrected lives. We can reclaim the promise that gives us life. We can walk again in paradise in fellowship with God our Father.

I now understood that it was never God's will for that child to have cancer, for any of us to suffer in any way. I wanted God to make it all right ... but he already had. We chose to make it wrong.

We all suffer. That's why God provided a Savior—to make it right again, offering us eternity in paradise by accepting him.

9

HAPPY FATHER'S DAY!

Our separation was very difficult for my aging parents. They loved us so much and hated to see any of us suffer. They also loved Tom and missed him. Understanding eluded them, too. Dad had an especially difficult time because memories of his own previous failed marriage, which had ended in divorce and separation from his two small daughters, became alive and hurtful once again. A lot of pain showed in his clear, light blue eyes.

We didn't talk about his first marriage. In fact, I didn't learn about it until I was a teenager, and it was a very traumatic truth for me to find that I had two half-sisters someplace. It's always hard for a child to understand. Sometimes there are no answers and sometimes even the questions are not well received. It was not possible for my dad to talk about his first marriage, and my mom and I honored that. I had always wanted a sister or a brother and to know that someplace I had two sisters was very painful for me, but, the necessity for my dad to keep that private was honored.

Dad had suffered a number of heart attacks, rallying each time to return home to remain with us a little longer. During this time, I had become very involved in church activities, desiring to learn more and more about God and learning about prayer—prayer for my marriage, my family. I was having wonderful experiences, which I shared with my parents and my friends. So whenever Dad became ill, I'd pray for his recovery and for his healing. I would call a group of people in my prayer group who devoted themselves and committed themselves to praying for special intentions. I would call and say, "Please pray for my dad's healing." And they would. I always knew and could count on that type of wonderful support.

Because I had been experiencing so many wonderful things and God was working so powerfully in my life and revealing himself so incredibly to me, I was asked on one occasion to share what is called in charismatic circles a *testimony* or a story of the involvement of God in your life. I was invited to do this for a "Life in the Spirit Seminar," a series of teachings to clarify who God is and his involvement in our lives—what he wants to do, what gifts he has for us, and how he wants to become intimately involved on such a personal level with us.

On this particular occasion when I shared my story, my message was taped. I took the tape to Mom and Dad's so they could really hear and understand how wonderful some of the experiences were. Even the ability and the experience of standing in front of and speaking to three hundred people was a miracle for me that I needed to share.

We three sat together listening and crying, reliving again the hurt, but also acknowledging the grace and wonder of what God was doing in my life. When the tape ended, Dad had a very pensive look on his face. He put his once strong arms around me and with tears in his eyes said, "A man has to do what a man has to do."

I said, "Yes, Daddy, it's okay." I knew he had come to a place of acceptance and forgiveness for Tom and for himself. Tom had been gone for three years now, but still I continued to hope and hold onto the belief that he'd come home.

I'd always been "Daddy's little girl." I wanted so much to please him, to make him proud of me, to be all he'd hoped for. He had always been such a wonderful example of the Golden Rule: "Do unto others." My dad was totally devoted to Mom and me. He was conscientious, warm-hearted, a tender and strong, honorable and righteous man. He was also very strict and very literal, not at all sloppy in his discipline. "No" meant "no," with hours of lectures to convince me of his wisdom and his expertise, to convince me that "Father really did know best!" It made following his direction easy. His way was always good, moral, kind, and difficult to dispute, so I didn't! It seemed to be the right way to live. We were very close.

From the time I was a little girl, whenever Dad and I parted, he always said, "Good night" or "Goodbye," followed by "I love you. Be a good girl!" My response was, "I love you, too. I will." Years and years of this departure blessed and reminded me that I was loved and I had an obligation. Two simple profound truths! How really profound this was to be to me, I was not to learn until after my dad's death.

NOT MY WAY

After playing my tape, I began packing my recorder, preparing to leave. We were saying our goodbye's, and I bent over to kiss Dad goodbye. He hugged and kissed me and said, "Goodbye . . .I love you." And I waited. I looked into my dad's face and waited for the other half of his message to me. I said, "Daddy, I love you, too. But what happened to 'Be a good girl'?" My dad looked deep into my eyes with so much love and pride. "You *are* a good girl," he said.

I would never hear my father say those words to me again. Soon after, my dad suffered another serious heart attack. I got the call from Mom, left work to drive one and a half hours to the hospital, and as I had done so many times before, I called my prayer group (the prayer line) to say, "Pray for my dad. Pray for his healing."

I jumped in the car to go to the hospital with a friend. We began praying as we drove, but this time there seemed to be a difference, a need to stop petitioning God and to listen to him. Over and over in my mind I heard the familiar words of Scripture, "Into Your hands I commend my spirit." A peace and assurance came over me.

"It's time, isn't it, Lord? It's time to let him go." I reached the hospital and saw my dad and mom. I then called the prayer line and I said, "Don't pray for recovery. Let him go. It's time." There was pain, but there was peace. I knew it was time. It was 1983, and my dad was eighty-five years old.

Daddy died later that night. It had been peaceful. It was finished. As Mom, my children and I were preparing to go to the funeral home, my youngest son said a beautiful thing to me, full of wisdom and truth. "Mom, isn't it wonderful of God to let you know him before he took Grandpa?"

"Oh, yes, honey," I said. "It is wonderful."

There was a terrible hole in all of our hearts. We all missed Grandpa. Mom especially, all alone now after nearly forty-five years together, was feeling the separation as I was. Hard times get harder sometimes. My dad died in March on St. Joseph's Day. Coincidence? I think not.

Soon it was June, and it was Saturday, the day before Father's Day. It was an awful day. I was missing my dad; I was missing my husband; and I was so angry at him for not being there with us. On top of all of this, I had a major argument with one of my children. It was the pits. When I wasn't yelling, I was crying. "Woe is me" was all I could feel. I was miserable and making everyone else miserable, too. I truly allowed myself the luxury of a major pity party and all were included. At some point, between the yelling and the crying, I remembered that this was probably not in God's most perfect will for me . . . and then the guilt hit.

The Sacrament of Reconciliation—confession —is a wonderful, healing gift of God's grace to his Church. Sometimes, and this was one of those times for me, it was a tremendous burden, the most unpleasant task that I could think of. I did not want to go to confession. I did not want to be reminded that I was sinning. I did not want to forgive anybody. Blaming everybody felt good. Yet I knew it was something I had to do. Yuck!

In this angry, crying state, I drove myself to church, slamming the car door as I left. I entered the church. Thank God there were only four others in the church and I could cry somewhat unobserved.

When it was my turn, I entered the confessional and began my tirade with very little repentance in my heart, if any. This was an exercise of my will and obedience. Of course, the priest knew me—it's a small town, and he knew my situation. But he also knew my heart.

"Andrea," he said with compassion. "You know what you must do."

"Yes, I know," I said stubbornly. "But I don't want to."

This was one of the very few times I did not feel loving towards Tom. I wanted to blame him for everything, even the fact that my dad wasn't with me. I calmed down a little and finished my confession. My penance, to forgive and to pray for my husband *again*, made me cry even harder. I did not feel like doing either!

I left the confessional still crying and blowing my nose. I went to the front altar and knelt there—so torn apart, so hurt by the argument with my son, so lonely for my dad, so angry at my husband, so utterly distraught.

I felt a hand on my shoulder and turned to face a woman who belongs to our parish, whom I knew slightly. She hesitated because I was still crying.

Finally she spoke. "I'm sorry to interrupt you, and I don't know how to tell you this," she said, "but I know that

NOT MY WAY

God wants me to say something to you. I keep hearing words that I'm to say to you. I don't understand this at all, but it seems like God wants me to tell you."

I looked at her, wondering what on earth she was talking about. "God wants you to tell me something? Okay. What is it? Tell me."

She looked at me again. "God wants me to tell you, *'Be a good girl!'*"

My heart pounded. I was overcome with awe. There was no way she could have known. So profound and precious a gift. "Thank you, Father."

"Happy Father's Day, Daddy. I love you."

10

MUCH AFRAID

Early in my walk with Jesus, a special book was recommended by a friend. The words grabbed at my heart as I recognized the main character. She was me. Her name was "Much Afraid" ... and I was! She lived in the valley of humiliation with her relatives, the Fearings, and she was desperate.

I knew that this was a story about me. I so completely identified with her that I could only read a paragraph at a time. I sobbed and sobbed. How could an author, whom I'd never met, capture my life, my pain, and my desperation so completely?

Hinds' Feet On High Places, by Hannah Hurnard, became my instruction book. (The title is based on the last verse of the prophetic book of Habakkuk in the Old Testament: "The Lord God is my strength, and he will make my feet like hinds' feet and he will make me to walk upon mine high places." —*Habakkuk* 3:19. A "hind," referred to in this verse, is a young deer—literally "one without horns"—that is particularly swift and agile, able to climb rugged mountain terrain with ease and grace.)

This book was an ongoing influence that changed my life, healing, inspiring, and directing me as I read it time and time again.

God's *Holy Bible* and *Hinds' Feet On High Places* helped me find my way back to life. From God's inspired Holy Scripture, I learned about him. From Hannah Hurnard's book, I learned about me. I was being taught how to leave the valley of humiliation and climb to the high places—the mountain tops, to freedom in the kingdom of love.

Much Afraid had companions to help her—to walk with her. They encouraged, supported, and loved her enough to enable her to change. Me, too! They were the acquaintances and friends that God continued to place in my life.

I began, as Much Afraid did, to attempt to follow the Good Shepherd. We were both almost too *much afraid* to try.

NOT MY WAY

She was an invalid, with crippled feet and a crooked mouth. I was an invalid, too. Unable ... disabled ... scared to death! But, I knew his voice. I had seen his face. There was no turning away.

As I read and tried to do what she did, the most amazing things began to happen. God manifested the same places and circumstances that were in the book. I couldn't miss them! They were *so* real. Similar events happened so often that I began to look for and ask for signs and confirmations from God ... and I'd get them, signs and wonders too marvelous for words!! I knew God was with me. He was pleased. I was, too!

I felt like a little child getting gold stars on a paper. My efforts were being acknowledged—like Much Afraid's, when the Good Shepherd looked at her with love and encouraged her to keep trying. God was encouraging me.

I talked to him.

I asked for his help.

I looked for him in circumstances and found him. I would wait for him when I didn't dare move. I would cry out in terror and feel him respond to me. I'd laugh sometimes and feel he was tickled and he'd nod his approval. When I got a little stronger and braver, I would expect him to show up, and most of the time, he would. Not always. We had to keep straight who was God. He'd wink at me. How playful and wonderful he was ... the most glorious love affair imaginable.

His love was unconditional—something I'd never experienced in my life. If I failed—if I fell short—he still loved me. He still wanted me. I was not scolded. I was encouraged. It was wonderful! And I was hoping that in doing this just right, I would get Tom back.

I continued to learn. It wasn't easy. Then, I began, as Much Afraid, to recognize behavior that was out of order. God calls it sin. With the strong light of God's truth shining on me, I could see it. It's one thing to recognize it; it's quite another to go through the excruciating process of eliminating it.

I knew I was loved by God. I knew he had placed companions and circumstances to effect my healing. I was secure enough in my relationship with him to continue the arduous task of change.

He is gentle and loving, even when he reveals sin. One

of the miraculous and wondrous things he does is ask permission to take it away. He woos and delights us to the extent that pleasing him becomes more important than continuing in sinful behavior.

I foolishly said, "Anything, God! I love you so . . . I've come to do your will!"

Dangerous, frightening statement! Of course his will is to heal sin and grant freedom and peace, but . . . to do his will required a death to my big, out-of-order self. Major conflict happens . . . wills collide . . . and a battle rages.

I know what Scripture means about wrestling with an angel . . . I wrestled with God. I ranted and raved, questioning, "What are you doing to me now? I've had enough! I don't want to be any better! I don't want any more healing! It hurts too much! Please, God, do it another way!"

But I knew there was no other way.

Every part of my physical, mental, and emotional capacity hurt . . . screamed . . . because I did not want to change. Change is not just a word. It's a reality.

The Good Shepherd, in *Hinds' Feet On High Places*, had Much Afraid construct altars of sacrifice where she had to put to death the part of her that kept her invalid, the sinful part. She had to come face to face with what it was—recognize it, identify it, and be willing to place it on the altar.

It's not easy to set down a part of yourself that has been with you for years, a character flaw that remains undetected until God's light exposes it. It takes courage and faith to let it go. It's scary to know you can't use it again as an excuse or a crutch. Standing on your own two feet is hard, seemingly impossible when you're crippled. But *nothing* is impossible for God. That is exactly what God required from Much Afraid to leave her pitiful place of humiliation, if she wanted the freedom to leap and run on the mountain tops with him.

That's what he was requiring of me.

As she climbed with her companions—Sorrow and Suffering—she encountered every terrifying inability and disability. Those attitudes presented themselves before her—monstrous, terrorizing, huge impossibilities. Mocking, torturing, hideous snarling voices held her captive and attempted to convince her that she would remain forever in their possession.

Her companions supported, assisted, comforted, and encouraged her. They enabled her when she was unable . . . altar after altar, time after time, sacrifice after sacrifice. Much Afraid would gather a small stone as the Good Shepherd instructed—a physical reminder that she had in fact overcome one more disability. I, too, gathered stones.

Much Afraid and I were inseparable. My companions helped as I climbed *my* mountain. It was better than being under it. Sometimes, though, I felt I stepped too close to the edge and was falling, hitting every jagged rock on the way down. I questioned, "Will I ever be able to accomplish this task?"

Little by little, I climbed higher than I ever thought possible. I could see better. I had a different perspective. My understanding grew. Things which had formerly loomed above me were now beneath me. Hindsight, as well as hinds' feet, were apparent. I experienced God's patience and mercy.

So slowly did I learn. So " much afraid" I was.

11

TOUGH LOVE

Crippling attitudes robbed me of health and freedom! They were extreme, sinful, and had to be changed.

After Tom left I occasionally sought the advice of a Christian counselor to help me with my low self esteem. When you've been rejected for no apparent reason and you're no longer loved, your worth is questionable. Mine was gone. I needed to learn how to value myself and trust my decisions.

My children had needed sound judgments and mine were shaky, to say the least. I had never been strong in the disciplinary skills. I'd always been the soft touch—less able to follow through with tough love.

Now, I had to. But I was also very much afraid of being too hard and being unreasonable. I didn't want to be too strict and lose my children. I was very confused.

I doubt if I ever would have been able to change if it weren't for my children and my love for them. They were so precious to me. Seeing their pain and confusion hurt me as much as my own. There was no way for me to protect them.

As they grew up, they struggled with their own difficult issues, as well as the pain, loneliness, and frustration in our family situation. Everything was magnified. Holidays were dreaded—not enjoyed. Birthdays and normal family celebrations were tolerated because forcing us all "to be together" was awkward and miserable.

There wasn't enough money to do the normal, everyday things without strain and worry. Disappointment was an expression I had to see on their faces over and over, year after year, and it hurt so much! I felt frustration and desperation.

At this time just one of my children still lived at home, and although he was working and out of school, I still needed to enforce house "rules." I had been advised by my counselor to stand my ground and address an issue with him. The outcome was worse than I'd feared, ending in departure from my home with the threat of never returning. I was devastated.

The timing of this encounter was not accidental. I was scheduled to attend an inner healing weekend the next day. As would always happen just before I'd go to an event or conference, a circumstance would present itself so I'd know what area God would be working on ... and it was usually very painful.

In this state of devastation, I drove to the retreat house, sobbing as I went, not knowing where he was. Upon my arrival, I was given a scripture—typed on my name tag—that I was to pray with and ask God to speak through. I was angry. The scripture was certainly not for me. It was: "If we confess our sins, ... "

I did not feel that I had sinned, but that I had been sinned against. I felt hurt and wounded and rejected. I was being left again. What had I done wrong? I'd always tried to be good and do things right and please people. I just could not comprehend what was happening.

I prayed and tried to understand. I cried and I was so angry at God that he had allowed this further pain. I did not like that scripture pinned on me about confessing my sins. The leader of the retreat, a Catholic nun with excellent gifts of inner healing, shared a form of confession that she had experienced at a conference for priests and nuns. She had learned to dance her confession, expressing with her body, as well as her lips, her sin. She and her confessor then danced reconciliation together. "How incredibly beautiful and profound," I thought, "to be so aware of my sins that I could express them through dance."

That night, as I unpinned my name tag and scripture from my shoulder, I prayed, "Show me my sin, Lord. Show me so clearly that I can dance it, that I can identify it, experience it, acknowledge it, know it, and lay it down with my whole being so I can express my total repentance to you."

Early the next morning, I awoke ... one word repeating itself over and over in my mind."

I heard "Abandonment. Abandonment."

"Yes, Lord, I know. I've been abandoned," I said.

"Yes, My child," he said to me. *"You have. But you, too, are guilty of abandonment. For had you not first abandoned yourself, you would not be so subject to abandonment. Your sin, my child, is abandonment."*

NOT MY WAY

Pain stabbed at my heart. I knew, to the deepest part of my being, that it was true. I felt remorse. I felt guilt and sadness. I felt overwhelming loss.

"Dear God. Yes," I said, "it's true." My mind was filled with understanding. I sat up in bed and slowly, deliberately stepped to the floor. I stood for a moment, heavy with the burden of this truth. I knew that I'd asked to know my sin so completely that I could dance it. It was not a pretty dance—but an honest one.

I could see myself as a baby—soft, pink, precious, a tender, fragile little girl child. I was beautiful. Then, with tears spilling from my eyes, I gathered myself in my arms. I held me. I loved me.

I slowly danced, holding the infant that was me. I bent and laid me on the floor in the corner of the room. I turned and left me there. I slowly, painfully danced away. From a distance, I looked back over my shoulder and saw, with horror, that I now resembled a starving, Biafran child. Wide, hungry eyes filled with the pain of abandonment stared at me. Guilt and awareness encompassed me completely. I rushed back to myself and stooped to gather me to my heart, never, never to abandon myself again.

"Forgive me, please forgive me," I sobbed. "I didn't know." I sat on my bed, slowly beginning to understand the enormity of what I'd just experienced: a profound awareness of how I'd lived my entire life.

The truth of that experience changed me. It revealed to me that my whole life was a compromise of bending, denying, lying to myself—of prostituting my needs, my wants—to do the will of another. In attempting to please everyone out there, I'd lost me. I'd never had the inclination, awareness, or desire to be anything but one who pleased others. I didn't know I had allowed it to become extreme and out of order. I didn't realize that to love and please anyone correctly, I had to love and honor myself first. I didn't know I had allowed it to become sin in my life, that in giving it all away, there was nothing left for me.

I shared my experience with the others at the retreat. We were all in awe of God's revelation. This profound experience of enlightenment and truth began my process of learning how to become me.

NOT MY WAY

My mind was full of what I'd experienced. Thoughts were clamoring for attention. Questions filled my mind. "How had this happened? What am I supposed to do? How can I change?"

I didn't know. My only certainty was that I needed help and information. I needed choices, so that I could learn to become me. It seemed silly, even a little embarrassing to admit that in my middle forties, I didn't know me. My entire focus had been, first, in pleasing my parents, then my husband, my church, my children, my neighbors . . . everyone.

"Who am I?" I wasn't sure. "Dear God, what do I do?" I was so frightened. These questions invaded my mind as I drove home.

Confusion gripped my heart as I remembered that my son, who had left home, might have returned. Before I had this new awareness, my normal focus would have been, "How could I please my son?" Now, because I questioned that, I didn't really know *how* I was going to respond. What was right? I didn't know.

Do I want to allow people to come and go in my life without my choosing when or where or if it's appropriate for them to return? This was a huge struggle for me. I was so willing to let people make their own choices.

I was torn. There was no car in the driveway. Disappointed? No. Relieved? Yes. No decision had to be made.

I was exhausted. I unpacked and settled in. I prayed.

The next morning, as I left for work, I walked to the car, locking the front door. "Wait," I thought. "That's not nice. What if he wants to come home and the door's locked?"

I got out of the car and unlocked it. "That's better, the door's unlocked."

And then I thought, "No. That's not right. I think I should lock the door. I think I should have authority over that door."

So I got out and I locked it. I got back in my car and I thought, "Gee. That really isn't very nice."

So I got back out and unlocked it. I got back in my car.

It took me seven times before I finally was able to drive away from my house with the door locked, realizing that it wasn't an awful thing that I was doing—that I wasn't really hurting anyone.

NOT MY WAY

"My house is finally being locked, and I really hold the key!" As the old doubts set in, I added, "... Maybe!"

God was showing me clearly that I had responsibility *for* myself and *to* myself to make decisions, to make choices. Yet, it was agonizing for me to say "yes" when I meant "yes" and "no" when I meant "no," to hold people accountable, to hold myself accountable. But I did.

As the days went by, I became stronger and stronger and felt more and more at peace with that decision. I locked my door every morning when I left for work, praying every afternoon when I came home that there would be a car in the driveway.

Three weeks went by ... it seemed an eternity. I trusted that I was learning and my son was learning, and I was right.

Finally, the car was in the driveway. I went inside, praying every step of the way. He asked if we could talk. I responded, "Yes, of course."

"I'm sorry, Mom. I was wrong. I should never have spoken to you like I did. Will you forgive me?"

"Of course I'll forgive you, but there are rules that must be followed if you are to live here," I said. "You are welcome as long as you understand that."

"I do, Mom," was the response.

I looked into his young, handsome face. We both had grown. I loved him so.

Our reconciliation was wonderful. The relationship was no longer on a level where I was afraid to be me, where I walked around on eggshells, not wanting to offend or punish incorrectly or discipline. It was a much more honest relationship that said "this is who I am" and "this is what I require" and "if it's something that you can honor, you're welcome to stay here; if it isn't, that's okay, too." Whew!

I was no longer terrified.
I wasn't uncomfortable.
I was a little afraid, but not *much afraid* ... finally.
Tough love is tough but worth it.

12

NEW WOMAN

My life was very busy. I was involved with two prayer groups and had resurrected my violin and played it for music ministry. I became a prayer group leader and also a leader in prayer ministry. I was growing in self-esteem, recognizing my giftedness and beginning to feel much better about myself.

I also found many opportunities to pray with my customers in the nursing home, which provided me with an incredible opportunity for healing and learning. Meeting and caring about people who were very ill and waiting to die was so difficult, and sometimes I didn't know if I could handle it. When my customers canceled, they really did! I know that death is not final, but a moving from a known place to a new, wonderful realm —eternity. However, watching the suffering and the fear of these elderly women and seeing the loss that families experience wasn't easy.

To me, they were the broken Body of Christ. Feed the hungry—those who can no longer lift a spoon. Clothe the naked—cover those whose arthritic hands cannot reach for their blankets.

I saw despair and depression. I watched as people rose above horrendous circumstances of loneliness and physical pain to smile and trust and love. I saw some give up and close up with anger and bitterness, denying themselves the grace and peace of a gentle passing. I saw the effects on families, the compassionate letting go of love, and the traumatic, frantic hanging on of fear. I learned more about kindness, touching and caring, hope, dignity and faith.

A lot of my judgments, self-righteousness, and pride were healed there. Truth was revealed and insights given. I learned that paralysis can be the prison of the mind, as well as the prison of the body.

Unlike the residents there who could not get well and recover and live productive and happy lives, I learned that, although my life was shattered and full of pain, it was not over. I could recover and I was "in process." I could learn to live again, to walk and run and dance, to enjoy my life. My thoughts, desires, and attitudes kept me crippled, though. How dichotomous. How perfect a place for me to learn to make choices that would allow life. I only worked there. I was free to leave.

God also placed some very special friends in my life there, precious people whose love I cherish. Their presence was a gift to me, but out of love and confidentiality, their stories cannot be shared here. They gave me life. They were also the Body of Christ to me.

Initially, *I* was the one who, in my pain and hurting, needed the nursing home, and I learned a lot about inabilities and priorities. Success in the world is often measured by titles, degrees, credentials, and well-educated minds, trained for a meaningful position. But that was not necessarily the case in the nursing home. Minds may not have had the experience of a formal education, but hearts were formed there. Touching and holding . . . the helpless found help . . . smiles and love were given away.

Soon, I became well enough to leave, and although I was struggling to make ends meet, I believed that God wanted me to stay in the nursing home. Believing that it provided opportunities for both my education and ministry, I continued to trust. My position there was a privilege and a faith walk, certainly not a prestigious position, but a calling. God provided so much more than money.

When my oldest son completed college, he found local employment and moved back home. It was great to have him there; he had been such an incredible support and I enjoyed having him close by with my other two children.

I'm not totally blind to the faults of my children . . . I'm sure they have some! But, as for many parents, the flaws are hard for me to see. They're wonderful people and I'm very proud and deeply grateful for their goodness.

He was working hard to pay his college loans and I was struggling on my nursing home salary and the few houses I cleaned. Groceries were the only way I could cut costs, and now, with a hungry young man to feed, I had to cook much differently.

NOT MY WAY

It was at this *inopportune* time that the Lord decided to teach me about tithing. I heard the word "tithing" everywhere—in teachings, on the radio, and in church. God requires our first fruits, our first ten percent of earnings, promising to return tenfold our offering, providing for and sustaining us.

God couldn't possibly mean me! I didn't even have enough for myself, and he wanted some? This was too much. I gave of my time, my talents, and my forgiveness—but I needed my pitiful little bit of money. *I* needed my "first fruits" . . . in fact, *all* my fruits to exist.

He was relentless, until one Sunday morning on my way to church, I succumbed to the pressure. "Okay . . . okay . . . okay . . . .*You win*!" I said reluctantly. My week at the nursing home had been very slow and my pay was sixty dollars. "If you think you need six dollars of my money, you can have it," I yelled. I begrudgingly placed six one dollar bills in the collection.

Angry obedience was the condition of my heart . . . far from the love, worship, and gratitude that tithing is supposed to exact from one's heart. I was still miffed when I returned home.

"What's for dinner, Mom?" greeted me when I walked through the door.

"Chicken." I said in exasperation.

"Mom, I can't eat another chicken. I just can't eat another chicken."

"I'm doing the very best I can," I exploded. "We are having chicken!"

My son put on his coat and stormed out of the house, slamming the door. My frustration reached its peak. "Why do things have to be so hard? What did I do to ever deserve this?" I cried, thoroughly giving way to self pity.

My son returned an hour later. "Cook, Mom, cook!" he said, as he placed bag after bag of groceries on my counter, the warm expression of love all over his handsome face.

I looked up in disbelief. When I emptied the last bag, I found the grocery receipt. An even *sixty* dollars was the amount! In less than two hours, my God had fulfilled his promise, using the generosity and giving heart of my son.

I continued to tithe, asking God in what area of the

NOT MY WAY

church he wanted me to give. A few weeks later, I felt his urging to sit quietly before him and listen.

"My child . . . I called you to give, to respond to me . . . to give to my church. You, my child, are my church. Take what you need when you need!"

I knew in this extraordinary way God had taught me to let go of more of my ways and my meager understanding. I experienced the reality of God's provision, as I believe King David did in Scripture when he and his men ate the forbidden *sho* bread in the Holy of Holies. I felt I was partaking from God's generosity, not my own efforts. How creative and profound are his ways; how tender and merciful.

The nursing home continued to hold unexpected blessings. When my mom's sister, my dearest Aunt Ethel, required extended care, I brought her there. She was an elegant lady; her body, not her mind, was her prison. It was excruciating to walk with this dignified woman into this place that she must now call home. She gripped my arm tightly, as we slowly walked the long hall to her room, fighting tears, almost losing her battle for composure.

She had unselfishly carried so many—her father, her mother, a sister, and brother-in-law. Now her back could no longer support even her own weight and she had to assume the humble posture of need.

In spite of all her pain, she managed to bring joy and love to a most undesirable situation. I was able to see her almost every day for the three and a half years she was there. I was privileged to be at her bedside when God took her home on Christmas Eve of 1991.

It was now 1987, seven long years had passed since Tom left. I questioned if my desire for reconciliation would ever end; I still loved him. However, after much prayer and difficulty, I finally agreed to a separation and divorce. I knew it was time for the legal closure to what had ended seven years before for Tom.

My daughter, who was now managing a health spa, called me with an incredible proposition. She was advised to hire someone to clean the spa and knew how much I needed money. It was a seven-day-a-week job offering excellent pay! I could clean it before and after work at the nursing home.

"Do you want the job, Mom?" she asked.

"Do I *want* the job?" I yelled excitedly. "Yes, I want it! I can do it. I'm not afraid of hard work; I need the money to pay my lawyer!"

I had been working very hard at becoming healthy, and having my own keys to a health spa seemed to me the perfect exercise! I polished mirrors, cleaned offices, vacuumed, scrubbed showers and bathrooms and then I used the equipment, enjoyed the sauna, and swam in the pool. How creative of God! I felt him smile and wink at me. How playful he can be!

On weekends, two friends helped me clean. Then, we all would enjoy the spa. One day, as I arrived at work, I *really* saw the name of the spa—the red, neon sign flashing at me—*New Woman*. I understood its message, reminding me who I was becoming.

"I got it, Lord." More *signs* and wonders. I laughed in appreciation.

How generous and creative is this wonderful Lord who had captured my heart, healing me in a nursing home, strengthening me in a health spa! I felt so blessed and loved. The creator of the universe, of the rivers and the trees, was courting me . . . wooing me . . . providing for and teaching me. I was in close communion with him. I was no longer dependent and needy.

I truly was a *New Woman*!

13

GIVE IT ALL TO JESUS

I loved music ministry. God gifted me with the ability to lead praise. I was involved in situations where the Catholic community came together for mass and special occasions where music was needed. I was the one with the microphone—arms lifted—praising my God. I was grateful, thankful, full of worship and awe, expressing my love to him through music, encouraging others toward an appropriate attitude of prayer and worship.

Our music ministry was invited to play for a week's mission presented by a Catholic lay evangelist named Charlie Osborne. Charlie presents his story in a dynamic and dramatic way of how Jesus touched his life and inspired him to change. His main message was, "You gotta give it all to Jesus." I was okay with that—I'd *already* given it all to Jesus!

I was confident. I received that message with a smug little grin. "Yeah, I've done it. I'm still standing." I nodded when Charlie brought up a point and I'd say, "Uh--huh! I relate. I understand. I did that!"

At this time, in my walk with the Lord, I felt secure. I didn't have much of anything left, and I was depending on Jesus to fill my every need. So, I could sit there and listen to Charlie's testimony and his message comfortably.

At this time in my life Tom and I were working on finalizing the divorce. We had each presented our lawyers with financial statements which had been given to the judge who would make his final determination. My lawyer assured me that I would receive a very generous settlement and maintenance. So, I was finally looking forward to a time when I didn't have to be so needy. The process required that we go to court, have a hearing, and finalize everything.

I was not going to court for anything that was out of order. I wasn't out to get Tom or to demand things that were unjust. But, I was finally able to recognize that I could ask for what I needed. It was okay. It was in order. Although I still loved Tom and didn't want this divorce, I knew it was appropriate. I had waited for nearly eight years.

I had been trying for all these years to build up enough courage, enough self worth, enough awareness of my needs to go to my lawyer and say, "This is what I need for my life."

I'd been working with the Lord on my low self esteem, my pathetic "anything-is-okay attitude." I was developing "Andrea" and finally was acknowledging that I had worth and dignity. I was gaining in integrity.

It was okay for me to ask for what I needed and wanted. It was a real struggle and it had taken many, many years and a lot of hard work for me to be *able* to say, "I need. I want. I require." And, it was okay that I required Tom to give them to me! So much of my life had been lived in trying to please Tom. His needs were first, mine second. This was my mind set when I went to Charlie's mission.

I had thoroughly enjoyed the first two nights of the mission. Charlie has an excellent way of presenting. He's an extrovert *par excellence* and I'm an extrovert. And . . . could I ever relate! I was *thrilled* with what I was hearing.

On the third night, though, I heard him say something a little bit different. Not only "You gotta give it all to Jesus," but a second message based on Scripture which I'd never heard before: "You don't take your brother to court."

Now . . . I *know* when the Lord is talking to me. My heart pounds. I feel fluttery inside. I have tears. I have cold chills. I feel his presence and I know I'm to pay attention. He's either teaching me, blessing me, or revealing himself to me. And I know, because it's happened so many times before, to listen carefully, to be aware of what's being presented to me.

Charlie reinforced this message, sharing phenomenal stories of how God touched the lives of people who refrained from going to court, when in the eyes of the world, litigation was justified.

This was making me *just* a tad uncomfortable, because *I* was scheduled to go to court. I was amazed at this message and at the timing of it for I had never been scheduled to go to court before! I definitely was not quite as comfortable as I had been the first two evenings of Charlie's mission. Over and over, he talked about this. I didn't like what I was hearing! My heart began to pound. Tears filled my eyes.

NOT MY WAY

"Don't teach me anything, God! I don't want to hear this. I don't want you to show me anything because I *want* to go to court to resolve all these issues."

I calmed myself with the rationalization that Charlie's message didn't really apply to me anyway since Tom was not my brother but my husband and it was okay to take my husband to court. Well, anyway, that's what I was trying to convince myself of.

Charlie persisted, nailing that message over and over to his audience. Jesus underlined it in red. I was infuriated! I didn't want to stay there . . . I didn't want to listen . . . I didn't want to be told that I couldn't go to court. I was trying to block out God and couldn't stand to listen to Charlie one more minute.

I jumped up and left, slamming the church door! I ran to my car, tears streaming down my face, and drove home sobbing, yelling at the Lord saying, "You can't mean this! You can't do this! You have taken seven years of my life to teach me that I have needs and wants! And now, you're going to tell me, 'I can't go to court to have them taken care of?' I can't do this, Lord! You can't ask this of me! This is too much! I refuse to listen to you!"

I wrestled with God all night. I agonized. I tossed and turned. I cried and begged. I pleaded, "Don't mean this. Please, Lord, don't make me walk this walk. I don't want to do this. I don't want to do your will here, if this *is* your will. You can't require it of me."

I got up the next morning with my face swollen, my eyes red. My son, Tom, said as he was leaving for work, "What's the matter, Mom? You look awful."

I began a tirade of what I'd heard the night before: about Charlie's testimony of total dependence on the Lord; of his faith, his assurance that God would take care of him; that Jesus was his Lord, his Savior, and his Master.

My wonderful son listened to me patiently, but this was one more difficult concept to grasp. I was yelling at my son, trying to convince not only him, but myself, that if God *truly* was my God, if my dependence and assurance was on him, and if my trust was in him, then I did not need to look to Tom for anything . . . no support, no money, nothing! I needed to depend on God alone.

Awful! This was difficult, terrible! Yet, I knew, deep

within me, it was right. God enlightens and requires different things of each of us. *This* I knew he was requiring of me.

I made my decision and told my son, "If Jesus Christ is to be my provider, I am not going to take your father to court!"

As he left for work, shaking his head in disbelief, he said, "You've *lost* it, Mom . . . you've *really* lost it."

It was difficult facing God. It was *very* difficult facing my son, who became more and more convinced that I had lost my mind. I sometimes wondered if I had, and yet, over and over, God showed me that I hadn't. He always provided a tangible reminder for an intangible truth . . . for something that I couldn't see, touch, or grasp.

By this time, I was a mess, so I went into the bathroom to brush my teeth and wash my face. I picked up my toothpaste tube and read it. Have you ever read your toothpaste tube? It said, "For best results, squeeze from the bottom and flatten it as you go up." I see God everywhere. He even speaks through a toothpaste tube. I know his voice.

"That isn't funny, God!" Yet, I knew he was speaking, showing me there was still some residue—my dependence on Tom. He was squeezing me, emptying me, and flattening me until there wasn't anything left. I had to give it all to Jesus.

I don't understand God's ways. I don't like them sometimes . . . a lot of the time. I went to the phone and called the church where Charlie Osborne was ministering. When he returned my call, I explained to him what was happening.

"Oooh, sister . . . sounds to me like God is doing a mighty work with you," he said confidently.

I asked if I could meet with him. He agreed.

I went with so many questions. He reassured me that I was doing the right thing. Charlie told me my faith and willingness to do what was required by God reminded him of his wife. He assured me, "God cannot be outdone in generosity, mercy, love, and tenderness. God will take care of you!"

I knew this, but I was still scared. I had walked seven years being taken care of by God and hoped it would get easier. Instead, I found that following Christ and obeying him sometimes get much more difficult.

I left Charlie, still feeling awful.

I called a close friend of mine. "I need to pray," I told her. "I believe God is requiring something *so* difficult of me that I need to know from him that it's true. I *need* to know on a physical, tangible level, that this is of God. I can't walk this, thinking that it might be an emotional reaction to Charlie's ministering. I have to know that this is God's will for me. If I'm not to go to court to get my needs met, then God has to meet them, and I need to know now!"

As I drove to my friend's house, I prayed a gut-wrenching prayer. "All right, God. If this is of you and you don't want me to take Tom to court, I won't. *But* . . . if I'm not going to have enough money to do the things I need to do, then *you've* got to provide what I need. And, right now, I need three pairs of off-white, sheer drapes for my living room so it will look nice for my daughter's wedding. If you provide them, I won't take Tom to court. And if you don't, I'm going! The only place I can afford to go is a garage sale, and that's where I'm going. Amen!"

I was devastated as we drove from garage sale to garage sale, finding nothing of use, certainly no drapes!

"One more garage sale and I'm going home *and* I'm going to court," I told my friend.

I turned around in a driveway in a very lovely section of town and noticed one more garage sale sign . "This is it. This is the last one. I'm only going here and then I'm going home. I'm exhausted!" I had a headache and felt awful.

We walked around and looked at the stuff. No drapes! Great! We started to get back in the car and the lady said, "May I help you?"

"No thanks," I said. "I don't see what I need."

"What might that be?" she asked.

"I need off-white sheer drapes."

"Come into my house," she said.

"Come into your house?" I asked incredulously, as my friend and I scowled at each other.

"Yes."

We walked into an empty room. My heart stopped. There were three windows—a double, a picture, and a single. They were lavishly draped with very expensive off-white sheers and custom side panels and valances. White isn't just white. There are shades of white. This was the right shade, *exactly* the right shade. I'm particular. These were the right sizes, too.

I looked at her and held my breath. My stomach churned. "How much?" I asked.

She responded, "Would twelve dollars be too much for all of them?"

I stood in the middle of her empty room, tears streaming down my face, and in awe, I raised my arms. "Praise You Jesus. Thank You, Lord. I'm not going to court!"

I was overcome with God's generosity, hardly able to speak! How could this be? How can I require so exactly from God and receive it?

Realizing that he had proven once more that he was so intimately involved in my life blew my mind! We drove home silently, totally in awe of his presence. I *knew* in the depth of my being that God was going to take care of me for the rest of my life.

As much as I was overwhelmed with his love, convinced of his will, and in awe of his grace, I still knew this was not going to be easy. I called my husband and said, "Tom, could you come over. I need to meet with you."

"Sure," he said.

He came over the next morning. I can still see him looking at me with utter disbelief as I explained about Charlie and his stories. Tom tolerated them for awhile. Then, as I began to speak about my personal experience with the drapes and that I believed with all my heart that God was going to take care of me, he listened intently. His face softened, and I knew he was listening to my heart and not just my words.

If I could take him to court, I would have some string, some control, some attachment to him. It would go on for as many years as it would take for him to maintain me. Releasing him would sever the ties.

How difficult it was for me to let him go. I still loved him so. I told him I would not need to take him to court, that God would provide for me. When you're holding on to somebody who's sinking or drowning, that moment comes when you know in your own strength that you can't hold them any longer. You let them go and you know when you do, that's it! That's the death—that's what it was like for me.

I let go. I didn't want to. I didn't want to go with God; I wanted to go with Tom. But I had decided to do God's will. I was making better choices for my life now, and this definitely was the right choice. How difficult it was for me to release him and let him go. I still loved him so. Yet, I knew he understood that I believed in what I was doing.

I looked at this man whom I loved. There were tears in both of our eyes. "I wish you well, Tom," I said through my tears. As he stood up to leave, we embraced, holding each other for a long time. I watched the door close as he left. It was heart-wrenching.

Later that day, I called my fine, Jewish lawyer to set up an appointment. I asked my friend to go with me and to sit in the outer office and pray.

"Boy, this is a pretty expensive decision I've made for you, Lord," I said to myself, but I knew it was right.

At my first appointment with my lawyer six years before, I was frightened and pathetic, telling him that I was a born-again Christian, depending on God for everything. He was tolerant and kind.

Now, over six years later, I sat opposite him about to tell him the same story, but I was no longer frightened and pathetic . . . I was sure.

I began to share with him Charlie's story. I included my own awesome story about my prayer and its answer—about finding the custom draperies for twelve dollars at the garage sale. I told him of my decision . . .

"I am not taking Tom to court," I explained confidently. "If I do, I would be limiting myself. God Almighty is going to take care of me. Not Tom."

His eyes never left mine as he shook his head in disbelief. He questioned me carefully, "Now . . . am I to understand that you're really not going to go to court? After all we've done for your settlement, you're not going to follow through with this?"

"That's right," I smiled and shook my head.

"I don't suppose it would do me any good to ask you to go home and sleep on this, would it?" he asked.

"No. No, it wouldn't," I replied.

"*How much did you pay for those drapes?*" he asked incredulously, leaning across his desk.

He stood up, gave me a hug, and said, "Pray for me."
"I will," I said. "Thanks."

What freedom there is in giving it all to Jesus.

NOT MY WAY

14

AMAZING GRACE

My mother, Grace, was born in 1900—one of seven girls and three boys. Extremely poor circumstances and hard times were her teachers. Her formal education ended in the seventh grade, when she was forced to leave to work in a laundry thirteen hours a day. An unreasonable, hard, strict father made growing up hurtful and difficult. However, she was blessed and influenced with a gentle, loving, faith-filled mother, who taught all of her ten children compassion and love.

As I reflect back, now knowing some of the extreme hardships they experienced, I have even greater honor and respect for their diligence and desire to become honest, hard working, productive people. They were an extremely close family who managed to create fun and hope in their dire circumstances.

"One of the most difficult things I ever had to do, Andrea," Mom recalled painfully, "was to go to the local bakery early in the morning with my little brother and wait outside until they opened, begging for day-old bread."

"Oh, Mom," I replied, "I'm so sorry! That must have been very humiliating for you!"

Mom maintained her dignity and pride throughout her life, though, and lessons such as this gave her the strength of character that made her a most amazing woman.

She married my dad in her mid-thirties and, hoping to start her own family, was devastated when told by doctors that her physical condition would prevent her from conceiving a child. Three years later, however, she was thrilled to find herself pregnant.

"You'll probably lose the baby," her doctor cautioned her. "And, even at best, you will definitely not be able to carry it full term."

Her response was simply, "What will be best for the baby? I can do it."

A full nine months later, a Caesarean section allowed a little girl's entrance into this world. Mom's change of life started

NOT MY WAY

at the same time, so I was it! The answer to all her prayers and dreams tied with a little pink ribbon.

The love lavished on me from my two adoring parents made responding to please them my nature. I was their priority. Material things and "goodies" were not important. They never owned their own home. My dad had one suit, which as I grew to be a teenager, I hated. My mom made most of our clothes. Modest was our existence. Hard work, honesty, integrity, and love was the language spoken at my house. Thank God.

I learned a lot about self-sacrifice and tolerance from my mom and dad. Phrases like "Do your own thing," "I deserve," and "Buy now, pay later" were unheard of by them. Patience, acceptance, and responsibility were taught, and my challenge became, "What can I do to improve my circumstances?"

Their love was constant and supportive—their reliable gift to me and, when I married and had children of my own, to all of us.

If that quality of parenting and lessons in living and loving were taught and received by everyone, this world would be a tender place in which to live. Peace would abound.

I was blessed in having my parents live close to me, only one-and-a-half hours away—far enough away for space and close enough for touching. They were both always there for us until my dad died. He was greatly missed by all after his death, especially by Mom.

Eventually Mom began to experience problems with her health, so I decided she should move closer to me where she would have minimal supervision and assistance if she needed it. Mom was a very independent lady, though. Moving in with me was out of the question, as far as she was concerned, since she considered it a burden to both of us. The local senior citizen housing offered by Catholic Charities provided a pleasant and safe apartment with other people her age whom she could relate to and enjoy. So it seemed the ideal arrangement, and the difficult but necessary move was made.

Wednesdays were our day. When I finished cleaning the spa at eight o'clock in the morning, I'd arrive at her doorstep, ready to clean her apartment and do the laundry as quickly as possible. Then, when the chores were finished, we'd head to a nearby mall for our favorite sport—shopping.

I learned well from my mom the art of good shopping. She was in her eighties and her energies prohibited marathon

NOT MY WAY

shopping, but two clever women overcame that little problem quite easily! We invested in a wheel chair which I would load in the back of the car, sit Mom in it when we got to the mall, and we were off for the day. What wonderful times we always had! She'd hold our packages while I'd wheel her up and down the aisles. She'd touch and handle things, not wanting to miss anything, and, occasionally, she'd try on clothes that I insisted she needed.

I'd ask, "Are you tired, Mom? Do you want to go?"

She'd look at me and smile and say, "No, honey, all I'm doing is sitting here. Let's keep shopping."

Her endurance amazed me, for our shopping trips soon turned into all day affairs. We'd do lunch, then later dinner, and, finally, get her groceries and head home. At the grocery store she bought three apple turnovers each week. She loved them. She'd cut them in half and have enough for six days. The seventh day, she'd do without. My mom's budget was also tight, and she was very used to portioning out just what she needed. There were no excesses in her life. She always had just enough. She was a gracious and wonderful woman. We all loved spending time with Mom.

When my daughter, Kelly, won a trip to Disneyland for her extraordinary sales ability at work, she called me with a proposition.

"Mom, let's take Gram," she exclaimed excitedly. "She's never been to Disneyland."

"Let's do it!" I agreed.

Among the many, precious qualities my daughter has are her generosity and thoughtfulness. She has always been perceptive and aware of peoples' needs and capable of meeting them.

"Gram, guess what? You're going to Disneyland!" was the way she extended her invitation.

Mom was thrilled. My children were the delight of her heart. With wheelchair, limited funds, and great expectations, three generations and a girlfriend flew to Disneyland. My daughter bought Mom a huge sombrero, rolled up her pant legs so she would get a tan, and, laughingly, we sat in the sun. What a precious time we had!

In Disneyland, there was no waiting in long lines. Mom, in her wheelchair, saw to that! We four rode most of the rides and saw the sights, and Mom even had a beer at Rosie

NOT MY WAY

O'Grady's. She never once complained of being tired. She was always a good sport and better natured than the rest of us. She loved to eat out, always taking a couple of extra sugar packets and fresh paper napkins "just in case." *In case of what,* I'm not sure. She hated to leave tips, thinking it was the restaurant's responsibility to pay their help enough.

Finally, we turned our weary but happy selves northward, back to snow and Christmas preparations. Mom had a window seat on the plane so she could see, even though cataracts made it difficult. She was so proud to be with us and made sure that she told everyone, especially the stewardesses on the flight, telling them she was eighty-seven and this was her first time flying. Our photos told the story of our wonderful time and she happily displayed them to her friends at home. She had a full and very happy heart.

A few days after we arrived home, Mom called. She had made a decision. She would give each of my children their very small inheritances before she died. She wanted to see their faces when they received them, so she asked me to fix a special dinner and invite them all so she could give them their presents. She received from their faces what she desired—love and love and love flowed from their eyes and hearts into hers. She was well pleased with her family and grateful for her full life. We, too, were so grateful for her.

Before Christmas, I had been thinking about how special she was to me, thanking God for her. When I felt inspired to write a poem telling her how much I loved her, I decided to frame it and give it to her as a gift. She loved it and, of course, shared it with all of her friends.

Little did we know that one month later—three days after her eighty-eighth birthday—she would fall and not recover.

How did the doctor miss the internal injuries? An oversight? Was Mom's death the result of an error in judgment? Or did God use this doctor's humanity and imperfection to answer the prayer that I'd said for so many years?

"When her time comes, take her quickly, my Lord," I had prayed over the years. "Not a lengthy, debilitating illness."

Did I blame the doctor? No. Did I accept that God took her home? Yes. God promises in Scripture to turn all things to the good. Some of the events in our lives are difficult to experience, but when you truly trust him, you can find acceptance.

NOT MY WAY

The calling hours at the funeral home were a celebration of my mother's life. My children and I chose a reasonably priced casket, knowing Gram would not have rested well in an expensive one. She loved a good bargain! I wanted to tuck in a sign just given to her for her birthday by her niece which said, "Out Dancing . . . " I believed she was!

I did her hair—she was beautiful!

My daughter put photographs from our wonderful Florida trip on a table. My oldest son bought eighty-eight long-stemmed red roses that were placed in elegant containers in front of her—a reminder of her grace and beauty.

My youngest son said to me, "Mom, you should read the poem you wrote at her funeral mass. Gram would like that."

"Moments of Grace"

This woman that you chose, My Lord,
The one to bring me forth,
Was chosen with great care and love
Prepared by you, of course.

The husband that you gave to her
Was surely heaven sent
To love, respect and value her
To live what marriage meant.

The joining of two separate lives
To grow and be together
To bring forth a tiny child
To love that child forever.

Conceived in mid-life was your plan,
Mature and full in heart,
This lovely woman, strong and wise,
For me was set apart.

She led me as a little child
To kneel to you for blessing
To care, to help, to love and learn
All about caressing.

NOT MY WAY

Her knowledge was of you, dear God
Your ways and wisdom learned
To value not the worldly things . . .
Real treasures were discerned.

She taught me how to recognize
Another person's fashion,
To understand his wants and needs,
To treat him with compassion.

Try not to judge or criticize,
You don't know his motivation,
To somehow recognize,
We are all Gods' creation.

It's taken many, many years
To truly grow in wisdom,
To know as truth the values taught,
To have a clearer vision.

To live each day throughout my life
With real love for another,
To care for someone else's needs
Was taught me by my mother.

I've learned all things are gifts from God,
They're called his special "Graces."
That's who she is, and that's her name.
My Mother is "God's Grace."

    The church was filled with love and tears as I read the poem. Our wonderful, amazing Grace! How sweet . . .
    Now, five years later, as I sit writing this chapter, I feel drained and spent; many soggy tissues hold the tears that remembering her wrench from my heart. The sun is hot here on my deck, taking what little energy I have left. I must lay down and rest.
    Writing this kind of book is like open heart surgery. I'm giving those who look a glimpse inside my heart. I'm open and vulnerable and in pain. Gathering my books, my Kleenex, and a tablet, I go inside to rest.
    First, though, I remember that I better water the hanging

NOT MY WAY

plants, baking and wilting in the sun, before I go inside to collapse.

Under one of the hanging baskets is my gardenia plant that I've been nurturing since I received it on Valentine's Day from Richard, telling him gardenias were my mom's favorite flower.

It's a difficult plant and had lost most all its leaves and looked pretty pathetic. I doubt that it will survive much longer. It has not bloomed.

As I walk over to water it, I do not believe what I see.
There, on the gardenia plant—one, small white blossom!
Grace? I think so . . .
Amazing Grace.

15
BACK ON THE CROSS

My greatest experience of Jesus Christ was through my own suffering. I'd met him there. I understood his cross in learning to carry my own. I also experienced resurrection from places and attitudes that were death to me. Many documented cases exist supporting the reality of a return from death, a coming back from a death experience. I had similar experiences, undocumented though, because my death was not a physical one in a hospital setting with witnesses and monitors to authenticate it. My "self" died, nevertheless.

The silent miracle of new life can occur only when the old life ends. Mine, with Tom, had ended and now, with Christ, I had risen above my circumstances and found new life. Sometimes, I felt God was asking too much of me, not necessarily in the experience itself, but in the accepting or forgiving of it. That's where my real death occurred. My will and my desire to withhold my forgiveness in certain circumstances were in direct opposition to God's requirement of me. At those times, I was required to "do cross time," as I now lovingly call it, to put my rigid, judgmental, unforgiving "self" to death ... *and* to embrace God-like attitudes and forgiveness.

I die hard—ranting and raving—unlike Jesus, who went accepting and forgiving to his cross. Forgiveness is the greatest obstacle in walking the Christian walk in human flesh, but it *is* the walk that proves the Christian. It's a difficult lesson. And, like Christ, I had to let go of my own will and say, "Thy will, not mine, be done."

Our Lord refers to the Christian assembly—those who acknowledge Jesus as Lord and Savior—as his body here on earth. We're called the Body of Christ—believers in Jesus, attempting to live according to his direction. He provides special people from that body who will share our hurts and our pain to help heal us. He knows the degree of trust, acceptance, intimacy, awareness, and love that's needed. Simon of Cyrene helped Jesus carry his cross, and I've been blessed with many such "Simons," too—friends who helped me carry my cross

NOT MY WAY

when the weight of it crushed and overpowered me, just as the original Simon helped Jesus.

Some very special friends now shared my life. We could talk freely and honestly with one another. Our level of trust and love was God's gift. We were all experiencing difficulties and receiving each other's support was a blessing. We met weekly and prayed with and for each other. Thank God for their friendship and support, for I was totally unprepared for what would unfold next in my life.

After my mom's death and following her funeral, my friends stayed and helped me clean up. I was exhausted when they left. I had been able to keep myself very busy with all the funeral preparations and things that one does when there's a death. It had all been so sudden and unexpected. Now, it was over . . . It was quiet . . . I was alone.

Eventually I fell asleep but was jolted out of my slumber a few hours later by a hideous nightmare. I awoke sweating, my heart pounding. I sat up and tried to rid myself of the dream but the feelings and the thoughts from the nightmare persisted—it was awful!

I couldn't escape the sickening and frightening drama going on in my mind. I was terrified, panicked, and reached for the phone. I needed help. What was happening?

When my friend answered, I sobbed, "I've had the most hideous nightmare and I can't seem to awake from it." I actually was shaking as I tried to explain it! I found I was still totally immersed in the nightmare, even though I was wide awake. My mind continued thinking unspeakable, horrendous thoughts! How could I be having a nightmare and be awake? It didn't make any sense. I was so confused.

My friend listened patiently and lovingly questioned me as I sobbed. I heard myself respond to things I knew nothing about. Answers were flowing from my mouth, bypassing my brain. What was happening to me?

Then, in horror, I knew these awful things were not details of a nightmare but *memories*. I was *remembering*, not dreaming! I felt like I was on a roller coaster speeding through hell. Memories, sights, sounds, smells came rushing back at me, clamoring at me, shouting their ugliness and revealing their hideousness to me! I felt physical pain! Revulsion! I felt nauseous! I felt detestable!

My friend prayed, trying to comfort me over the phone,

NOT MY WAY

as I cried and talked in disjointed sentences. Sobs and moans filled the quiet night as I continued to see fragmented pictures. They exploded in my head! It seemed like hours before I was somewhat calm.

I remember my friend saying, "I'm coming . . . I'll come over. You'll be okay. I'll be there."

I was afraid to hang up the phone. As I waited, excruciating memories kept spilling and tumbling into my mind. I realized, with horror, what had happened.

When I was a small child, living with my grandparents, my grandfather—in his senility, in his sin, in his pervertedness, in his own woundedness—had abused me. I was sickened.

When my friend arrived at my house, he called Father Regis and asked that we be covered in prayer. Father assured us that he would come over as soon as he could.

One of his greatest gifts was inner healing and praying people through situations and memories that needed the loving touch of Christ. Father Regis, another precious and gifted friend, and I were prayer partners in inner healing, and people came to *us*, sharing their most intimate tragedies, their deepest woundedness. We prayed for God's mercy and compassion and provided a safe place for them to be healed.

I felt compassion and empathy for the women I prayed with who had been sexually abused. Never in my greatest imaginings would I have thought that I was one of them. I now understood the level of my compassion. A friend once said to me, "I wondered if you were one of us because the tears that you shed with us must have come from a place of real knowledge." How well she knew. How little I knew. Unknown even to myself, I did have *experience* in this ministry!

Now . . . it was *my* turn.

I was filled with such repulsion—such shame. Words like *incest, sexual abuse, violation, defilement* were no longer just words. They were . . . emotions! They were . . . pain! They were . . . feelings! They were . . . horrifying! They were real!

For you who have been sexually violated, I need not say another word. For those of you who have not, mere words are never enough for understanding.

I had heard about people blocking memories, that a defense mechanism built within our psyche allows us to escape from circumstances that are too horrifying to accept. Memory

NOT MY WAY

reoccurrences and flashbacks *do* happen and are very, very *real*. I couldn't believe that within the boundaries of my *perfect* family and my *perfect* background, I was a victim of sexual abuse. My parents were so loving and protective of me, their only daughter. My grandparents adored me. This simply could not have happened to me!!!

It took days . . . weeks . . . months . . . years . . . of prayer to deliver me from the effects of sexual abuse.

Initially, I was grateful for God's timing . . . thanking him for his mercy and compassion of waiting to reveal this hideous truth after my mother's death. After all, it was *her* father who was the abuser, my grandfather!. As a family, we had been protected for all those years, as long as my mother was still alive.

But, as time passed and healing continued, much of my anger and rage was directed toward God. "You *loved* me, God, and you *allowed* this? This is *how* you love me?" I ranted. "What kind of God are you? You hold me in the palm of your hand . . . and *this* goes on there? I hate this! Why??? Why didn't you stop it?"

For weeks, I raged!

"How did you allow all those loving people—my mother, father, grandmother, and aunt—to be so blind? How could they not see what was happening? I was too young to articulate sentences or to even understand moral issues. Why didn't someone see? Where were you?"

Abusers are sick people, with extraordinary abilities to cover and deceive—to protect themselves. Innocent people become victims of their sickness. Hideous, but true. What lies were whispered in my little, innocent ears I'll never know completely.

Through this most difficult experience, I learned about God's greatest gift to us—our free will! How, once given, he leaves it with us—all of us. Some misuse the gift and horror happens. Sin and atrocity claims victims. How fragile we all are. How desperately we all need a Savior.

Questions that my conscious mind could not formulate and reasons for certain behaviors of mine soon became crystal clear. For instance, I have always thought of intimacy and married sex as wonderful, a blessing and a gift, as long as they were in proper order with love and goodness present. It's what I call "out-of-order" sex that has always revolted me. Lust, dirty jokes, perverted stories, expressions of sexual mockery and sexual insinuation had always affected me to an *extreme* degree. I always would catapult myself out of a situation where immorality was present and run to a place of morality and safety. I had always found it difficult to be neutral in such situations and was very judgmental and opinionated.

I thought that I found these occasions repulsive and offensive only because I was a moral Christian. Now I understood the real reason. I *realized* that these obnoxious, perverted situations came too close to the truth, and I was not ready for it to be revealed.

My awareness of the sexual abuse answered questions and clarified some other behaviors, too. Subservience, my desire and need to please, and my sense of inferiority and inadequacy now became understandable. I had always bowed to male authority. Now I understood the root cause. I was taught at such an early age. My powerlessness and fear, my feelings of being disabled and unable in many circumstances all made sense to me now, as did my worthlessness, low self-esteem, and dependency.

A major piece of the puzzle of my life, one that I didn't even know was missing, slipped into its key position and interlocked with so many other pieces of my past, creating a clearer and more complete portrait. Sexual abuse confuses boundaries in relationships. It oversteps them . . . overrides them . . . eliminates them, in many cases. Respecting space and personhood gets lost. Sexual violation did this to me!

Prayer led me to a gifted and compassionate woman counselor with whom I could share my experience more intimately, whose expertise answered questions and presented solutions and choices for my life. She showed me that the sanctity of my personhood had been violated, my innocence robbed!

Now that I was aware of this atrocity, I questioned my ability ever to be completely intimate again, and she assured me, in time and with hard work, I would be okay.

A lot of distorted feelings and mixed messages occur with sexual abuse, causing great mental confusion, especially to a child too young to distinguish acceptable from unacceptable touching.

Through it all, my dear friends, my "Simons," helped me carry my cross. Their concern, love, and patience healed

NOT MY WAY

me. They spent hours and hours listening to me, letting me cry, letting me be angry, letting me express the horror. They were *truly* the Body Of Christ!

I learned about forgiveness. I learned that forgiving *once* doesn't do it; that God really knew what he was talking about when he said, "You must forgive seventy times seven." As each memory appeared and reared its ugly head, I needed to forgive . . . again and again and again. It seemed like far more than seventy times seven.

I had to forgive God first . . . then, everyone else. Initially, my forgiveness was merely an act of obedience. I forgave because I knew that I *should!* But I didn't want to. Little by little, I experienced the process of genuine forgiveness, not just mouthing the words, but feeling the feelings, crying the tears, screaming the anger, shouting the questions. Then, understanding began to accompany and enter in until, finally, I came to a place of genuine forgiveness and love. It took a lot of time and hard work.

To me, this was my crucifixion. I did a lot of "hanging on the cross," a lot of "dying" to the resentment and injustice, and a lot of emotional "bleeding."

The thoughts that pierced my mind with agonizing pain as memories returned became my "crown of thorns." My garments of protection and denial were stripped away, leaving me in shame . . . until finally, there was nothing for me to do but to give it up and say . . .

"Father, forgive them, for they know not what they do."

16

NOT MY WAY

In my intense prayers for my family, I had included my father's former wife and their two daughter even though I had no idea who they were because I had no names. My father's family was all deceased and I accepted the fact that I would never know them.

One day, in sorting through old papers of my mom's, I discovered an address book. In looking through it, I found a name that I remembered, a cousin of my dad's, whom I had met when I was ten or eleven. Her phone number was there and I was instantly intrigued.

"I wonder if she's alive?" I questioned.

She must be quite elderly. I wonder if she'd remember me? I wonder if she knew about Dad's first marriage. (It had been a subject no one ever talked about.)

I decided to call the California listing and although the phone rang, no one answered. I tried numerous times over the next few weeks without success. I gave up trying.

Then early one afternoon, as I walked past my phone, I felt an urging to try again. I looked up the number, dialed it, and someone picked up the ringing telephone three thousand miles away.

"Hello," said the voice, much to my surprise.

I spoke her name and she responded, "Yes?"

I told her who I was and immediately she said, "Oh, you're Bill's daughter. I remember you, sweetheart. It's been so many years. Your mother called me when your dad died, but I haven't heard from her in years."

I couldn't believe it. I told her about Mom's death and that I'd been trying to call for a long time but no one answered.

"Oh, you know dear, I'm in my eighties, and I'm very busy. I belong to the Baptist church and there is just so much to do. I'm rarely home."

She then began to share about her full and marvelous life which included her work in the church. She had supported numerous children from all over the world, keeping in touch with them. They were all her family, for she had no children of her own. She had the world's. What a remarkable woman!

I courageously asked if she knew about my dad's first marriage.

"Oh, yes, sweetheart!" was her response. "Phyllis was here just last summer. Let's see, she'd be your half-sister, right? She lives in Canada. Her mother and her sister died many years ago, though."

Tears were dripping all over the telephone as I listened to her tell me about my sister. Phyllis was thirteen years older than I. It was amazing. I heard about her when I was thirteen and she heard about me when I was born—she was thirteen, too.

"I have her number if you'd like it. You should give her a call. I'm sure she'd be happy to hear from you," she continued.

After a long conversation, we hung up. My emotions were running rampant. Happy, sad, elated, scared . . . Could I just call? How could I do this? What would I say? Would she even speak to me? Would she be happy . . . resentful? I was a basket case.

After many minutes of anxiety, I decided to pray. I began *"Our Father . . ."*

Those two words said it all.

They were our father—God and Dad. I had never been able to call my dad "our father" with anyone before. Now, someplace in the world was the person I could say "our father" with—my sister.

I was sobbing again. When I quieted down, I gathered all my courage and went to the phone to call her. A man answered. Holding my breath, I asked to speak to Phyllis. An eternity passed.

"Hello," she said.

"My name is Andrea," I said. "I'm Bill's daughter," speaking his full name.

There was silence on the line.

She finally spoke, "Then, you're my little sister."

"Yes . . . yes, I am," I cried.

I really don't remember what transpired next. We were both so excited. But we talked for a long, long time and made plans to see each other.

The next weekend, a friend drove with me to Canada and after fifty years, I met my sister. She was absolutely wonderful

NOT MY WAY

and so was her family. I met her husband, children, and grandchildren. I had pictures of our dad, and we kept interrupting each other in our exuberance to share our stories. My greatest disappointment was that I'd never met Mary, my other sister.

Phyllis and Bill are devoted Christian people. They're Baptist, like our dad—I'm Catholic like my mom. Our love for Christ overcomes any differences. Our Father truly *is* our father.

How extraordinary it was to discover my new family. It became more and more apparent that God was healing my family. His timing is perfect!

This was the awareness I had when a month or so later my prayer group invited the author of *Healing The Family Tree,* Doctor Kenneth McAll, to minister at a healing Eucharistic celebration. I was privileged to prepare dinner for this gifted English doctor, Fr. Regis, and two other prayer group members, where he shared his personal miracles and powerful ministry which God had provided for him.

He taught us to bring to Christ, in the celebration of the Eucharist, all family members who lived and/or died in unusual, extreme, sinful, or violent ways who remained outside the family's forgiveness. Instances of suicide, murder, miscarriage, or abortion could all be healed in this manner. He taught that our forgiveness releases others from spiritual, physical, and emotional bondage, enabling them to live free lives in Christ.

He taught that generational healing was necessary to bring wholeness to the family. Scripture refers to the sins of the father being passed down through the fifth generation. Doctor McAll's belief was that through forgiveness and the celebration of Holy Eucharist, sins could be atoned for, thus stopping intergenerational bondage. Doctor McAll's ministry amazed me: one more revelation to me of God's limitless and profound *ways*.

My desire was to pray in this manner, especially for my grandfather, bringing him in my personal, loving forgiveness to Christ, putting in right order the effects of his sin against me; setting him, myself, and my children free... free from the sin, the anger and resentment, and other residual emotions and attitudes that lingered and could imprison and claim even more victims. How phenomenal to pray in this manner! It's referred to by Doctor McAll as healing the family's roots. The "tree" bears the fruit that originates in its roots.

NOT MY WAY

I began to pray for my family in this way. I attended daily mass, mindfully commending to Jesus my entire family and my husband's family, naming all those whose problems I knew and forgiving them in my heart.

Doctor McAll also taught that we could pray for our miscarried or aborted children, recognizing in a deeper way that they too are family members in broken relationship—not just unborn—but often times, unnamed and unmourned.

I had experienced a miscarriage after my second child. It was a difficult pregnancy and at the end of my third month, I miscarried. I dismissed from my mind that my *child* had died, recognizing only that I'd had a miscarriage. My knowledge was limited and my grief inappropriate.

My eyes were now open and I realized that I'd never even acknowledged my precious child as I would have if I had not miscarried. I asked God to reveal to me if my child had been a girl or a boy. We did not have the availability of ultrasound, then, and I had to rely on God's revelation.

"A little girl" was his answer to me.

"Lord, you tell us in Scripture that you call us by name. What do you call her?"

"Sara Elizabeth," he said.

When she had a name, it was as if the floodgates of my "mother's heart" opened and I grieved. I never looked upon her face. I never inhaled the sweetness of her. I never held her. I could feel the ache in my heart and in my arms. That empty place ... was Sara's. How sorry I was! In my ignorance, I had not even recognized my own precious, baby girl.

As I prayed in daily mass for her, my grief was healed and was replaced with joy. I knew she was with her real Father—Abba, God. His purpose for placing her within my womb, I'll never know. I'm just thankful he did.

I continued to pray for my family. And as usual, God showed me in extraordinary ways, using ordinary circumstances, that he had heard and answered my prayer.

For me, this is a valid way to pray, and God confirmed this once again through an experience with my youngest son, who was having a lot of trouble with his teeth. X-ray's showed that he needed some major work done. Cavities, filling replacements, and three root canals were scheduled ... much to his and his wallet's distress.

I was at work in the nursing home when he called. Of

NOT MY WAY

course, I had been praying for him. (Although my children sometimes thought I was a little—a lot?—weird with all this "God stuff," they did ask for prayer).

"Mom," he exclaimed. "You won't believe it. I was at the dentist's and he began drilling my tooth that needed a root canal. He was puzzled to see it was okay and only needed to be filled. Then, as he began to prepare for the second root canal and found the same thing, he said to me, 'That's *really* strange.'"

"Mom . . . he asked me if somebody was praying for me. I told him you were and that you always do."

"Then, he began the final root canal and you won't believe it! It only needed to be refilled. The root canals, even though seen on the x-rays, weren't necessary. He said, 'This has got to be some kind of miracle or something.'"

My son was elated. No pain for either him or his wallet!

"That's my kind of miracle!" he said. "Thanks, Mom. Thanks, God! That's great!"

Of course, I was thrilled.

"Alleluia! Praise You, Jesus!" filled the beauty shop in the nursing home. Passers-by were not really surprised, for I was known there as the "Jesus freak" . . . a title I loved.

I was bursting with joy and had to share this great news with a friend. So I called her and through "Praise you, Jesus's" and "Thank you, Lord's," I explained to her what had happened. It's fun to be charismatic! It's great to allow all that exuberance to spill out of your heart and mouth! I personally get more excited about God's *touchdowns* than mere football games or man's accomplishments. "Yeah, God!!!" She joined in my cheerleading—"Praise you, Jesus!!!!!!" I needed to return to work so we hung up and explained to my customers what the celebration was all about. The beauty shop was full of joy as God once more provided.

Minutes later, she called back.

"Andrea," she said almost in a whisper. "The roots . . . your family's roots . . . you've been praying for in daily mass. The roots are healed," she said with profound reverence.

Later that evening, I thanked God properly. My elation turned to awe as my God once again enfolded me in his loving presence. I was in holy communion with him. My spirit swelled and became one with his overpowering love. I experienced Mary's joy as I prayed my own *Magnificat* . . . "My spirit

NOT MY WAY

rejoices in God my Savior ... For he who is mighty has done great things and holy is his name."

My love spilled from the deepest places of my being as I realized the fullness of the healing of my family roots. Words paled but expression was needed. I sang the *Sanctus*: "Holy, Holy, Holy ... Lord God of Hosts ... Heaven and earth are filled with your glory! Hosanna in the highest!" My own words of praise and love flowed forth:

"I love you so, my Lord," I said. "I love you, Holy Lord. I am in awe of your generosity. I am in awe of your ways. I keep falling more and more in love with you, Jesus. I say, 'Yes, Lord' ... I will be your bride. Make me pure, Lord, cleanse my garments. Make me worthy. Call me forth. Use your servant. I am yours, Holy Jesus. Clothe me in white robes of righteousness. Tie me around with heavenly blue. Adorn me with gold and precious jewels. Make me a bride worthy of her husband ..."

Without realizing it or planning it, my prayer took on a poetic form ... and, as I prayed, I continued writing:

> *Take me where you will, Lord. Have your way with me.*
> *Empty me ... or fill me ... Lord, to all eternity.*
>
> *Mountain tops or valleys, floods or gentle rain,*
> *Deserts or oasis, with you its all the same.*
>
> *Blessed Holy Savior, owner of my heart*
> *Precious Holy Jesus, we will never part.*
>
> *Thank you for my freedom, thank you for the dove.*
> *Holy One, Redeemer, thank you for your love.*
>
> *Abba, Abba, Father ... fill me with your grace.*
> *Abba, Abba, Father ... till I look upon your face.*
>
> *The Alpha, the Omega, the first and the last*
> *Everything completed, the future and the past.*
>
> *Help me walk it straight, Lord ... guide my very path*
> *This way that was not my way ... will be my way at last!*

NOT MY WAY

My heart, my spirit, and my mind were filled with his sweetness. It covered me in lavish abundance. His personal involvement in my life continued to astound and bless me.

How could I not believe that God loved me? How could I doubt his faithfulness? It was at times like this that my "yes" to him was heartfelt. The desire in me was to become all he desired. We were in agreement.

Jesus says in scripture, "Where two or more agree . . ." and we do—God and me! There can be no better way to live my life than to live it . . . *his* way.

17

HINDS' FEET—I GOT 'EM!

When my spiritual director, Fr. Regis, was assigned to a different parish, I felt a great loss. He had not only been mightily used by God for my healing but also was a very dear friend.

I was now in active ministry and felt the need to be under the headship, guidance, and authority of my parish, and with Fr. Regis gone, I asked our new parish priest, Fr. Ralph White, to be my spiritual director. This decision proved to be another of God's most powerful and precious gifts to me, for Fr. Ralph's direction was exactly what was needed. His relationship with God and his incredible giftedness in prayer continued the work of cleansing and healing.

One day, at the beginning of my period of spiritual direction with him, Father Ralph called to say that the Lord had given him a message for me, that I was to be called by a new name, "Glory." Father Ralph had no way of knowing the significance of the name Glory, for I had not yet shared about my identity with the book, *Hinds' Feet on High Places*. As Much Afraid overcame her disabilities and inabilities, she was given a new name, too. The Good Shepherd called her "Grace and Glory." I knew Fr. Ralph's call was a direct message from God. I knew that he was the holy instrument that God would now use to draw me ever closer. We, too, became partners in healing and good friends.

All too soon, Fr. Ralph was transferred to another parish. However, I felt led to continue under his direction and traveled one-and-a-half hours to the beauty and tranquility of the Adirondack Mountains, where I walked in the woods, sat for hours in the chapel, and received profound wisdom and direction. Since God always worked in the physical realm with me so that I could touch and see his gifts to me, I also believed that God had called me there to the mountains, as he had called Much Afraid to learn to attain the high places.

I learned about a special ceremony available in the

NOT MY WAY

Catholic Church called the *Enthronement of the Sacred Heart of Jesus*. This powerful and prayerful ceremony publicly acknowledges one's intention to have Jesus Christ honored as Lord of one's home and family, deepening the awareness of his presence in our lives. I scheduled the enthronement in my own home, inviting a few close friends to celebrate this occasion with me. The service was beautiful and when it was over, the presenters reminded me that confession would be an appropriate conclusion to the enthronement, preparing not just my home for God but cleansing my house within as well.

I believed special, spiritual graces could be obtained by a thorough examination of conscience and a complete and mindful confession. My desire increased to come before God with true repentance in my heart, acknowledging my sins and changing detrimental behavior to become healthier.

I called Fr. Ralph to make arrangements the next weekend for a private prayer retreat. I told him of my purpose—to make a good confession.

It was always a joy for me to go to the mountains to pray. My spirit found peace and contentment there. My journey to wholeness became so manifest there in the mountains. They helped me to grasp the concept of what I was doing—climbing to the high places with the Good Shepherd.

Fr. Ralph called back .... "Glory . . . ," he said, for that's the name he called me now, recognizing the profound similarities between my life and Much Afraid's. He knew God used that book as a powerful tool to teach me.

"Glory . . . bring your hiking boots. I've found a special place and I'll hear your confession there."

He would not tell me more.

On the drive to the mountains, I prayed "Let me know my sin, Lord. Help me to make a good confession."

Sensing that this was not going to be a usual confession with my grocery list of "no-no's" but something much deeper and profound, I found myself a little uncomfortable and apprehensive. I know when I ask God to reveal my sinfulness to me like this, he does! He understands my heart better than I. He knows when I'm ready to change and grow. I believed this was one of those times. It felt important.

Sitting alone in the small chapel I prayed and tried to listen to God speaking to me. This time I didn't really know what to confess—what attitude or action to change. This felt

NOT MY WAY

different. Hours went by. I still didn't know what I was going to say in my confession, but somehow I felt ready.

"Okay, Glory, get your boots on . . . Let's go!" said Fr. Ralph with a smug little smile on his face.

We drove a few miles and parked the car next to a sign marking a trail up the mountain.

"I found this place awhile ago," he said, eyes twinkling as he grinned at me. "Follow me."

It was a bright, sunny day, and the woods were cool. As the sun broke through the trees, playing on the narrow path, its rays warmed and welcomed us. How beautiful it was!

As we climbed, so did my sense of anticipation and excitement. Soon, I heard a faint and unfamiliar sound that grew louder and louder as we continued our ascent. Then, as we rounded the trail, we entered a clearing, and directly opposite us, on a cliff, was a lovely, cascading waterfall. Its beauty captivated me! I looked with awe at this unexpected wonder. The dancing, spilling water, the sun glistening on the wet rocks, the lush green of the ferns and trees, the scent of the pines . . . it was breathtaking!

"Oh, Father," I breathed. "How glorious!"

I sat down on a large rock beneath a towering pine and looked up at the waterfall. I was surrounded with beauty. I remembered Much Afraid. Her heartbreaking journey had led her, also, to a waterfall. There the final death of her will occurred—her hopes and dreams for human love were sacrificed as she courageously chose to do the Shepherd's will. Her climb had been done in faith, for she still did not have her hinds' feet and had not yet attained the high places.

"Pray," said Father gently . . . "I'll be back."

I was all alone in this most wondrous place.

"Dearest, Lord," I prayed. "I do not know what sin to bring to you. I cannot name it, for I really do not know it. Please, my God, help me to know. I do not understand my sin and I desire to give it to you."

My eyes were drawn to the top of the waterfall, the mist and spray softening its edges. Clearly, as if hung from the heavens, I saw a word. It seemed suspended above the waterfall.

Dependence. The word *dependence* filled my sight.

I gasped at the revelation and was immediately aware of its meaning.

NOT MY WAY

"Yes! Yes! Yes!" I cried to God. "My sin *is* dependence. I was truly unaware that I had choices other than obedience. I was too much afraid to trust myself. I was fearful of not pleasing those whom I loved and ended up dependent on their choices for me. I lacked the courage to walk independently. All my life, I've been dependent. This is the way I've lived. Always existing by relying on someone to support me—to carry me emotionally. I've held on for my life . . ."

In that brief moment, the eyes to my understanding were opened wide and I recognized the truth of my dependent behavior. How extreme and out of order it was, like the crippling of Much Afraid. My dependence kept me from standing tall on my own two healthy feet. My attitude was one of dependence, and my dependent attitude was my sin.

God wanted me free, not dependent. The truth of the statement, "We are what we believe" struck and stung with accuracy. In my belief that I *could not* be anything but dependent, I really, actually, could not! My negative and false self-belief had robbed me of my freedom!

How perfectly appropriate that God had me climb to this place beside the waterfall to let go of this crippling behavior. How wondrous to bring me beside living water to wash away my sin.

Fr. Ralph appeared, somehow sensing that I was ready for my confession. We walked to the waters edge and sat on two large rocks. Father sat opposite me. I looked into his eyes as I confessed my sin of dependence. Tears rolled down our cheeks as we both knew God had clearly spoken. I would be crippled no longer.

At the end of my confession, he reached into his pocket and pulled out a pix—the small container used to carry the consecrated host, the body of Christ, to the homebound or hospital patients who wished to receive Holy Communion. When he opened the small silver pix, I gasped. God's presence was released from the container that held him and he stood before me in all his majesty and grandeur. For one brief moment, I beheld the wonder, the fullness, of God. I recognized him to be all he's ever said he is. I felt his incredible mercy and compassion. I experienced absolution and love. I truly experienced Holy Communion, the real presence of God.

Fr. Ralph left me alone.

NOT MY WAY

I was awe struck . . . without words . . . overcome with humility and reverence, exquisitely aware of God's presence and his gift.

Fr. Ralph returned and we silently made our way back to the car, acutely aware of my miraculous experience.

God's revelation to me was profound.

His truth changed me. I was to be free in my relationships, no longer dependent in them.

I had my hinds' feet. I could walk on my own. I eventually learned that interdependence is the goal in human relationships—leaning into one another to touch and love and support, while maintaining healthy space and independence.

Our dependence belongs to God alone. Only he is equipped to lift and carry us. "Come unto to me, all who are weary and heavy burdened, and I will give you rest."

18

I ATE THE CARROT!!!

My belief was still that God would miraculously heal my marriage. Although I was divorced, that legal piece of paper did not change my heart. I still loved Tom and in spite of all the years and all the circumstances, I wanted him for my husband. I believed with all my heart that God would not have told me that Tom would come home if he had not meant it. I just had to wait it out!

For years, I'd placed that intention for a miracle in every petition basket, requested it of every prayer team, and took that spoken hope to every conference. I had every priest and person I knew praying. I believed it was right and so did everyone who prayed for it.

What kind of sense does it make that God would heal a man with cancer and return him to his family and not heal the marriage? It made no sense to me.

I held on stubbornly with both fists to the words that God spoke to me the very first time I heard his voice so many years ago: *"Tom will die to self, my way, my time." I* believed so completely that those words meant that my marriage would be healed that nothing could convince me otherwise. God had spoken!

I continued to walk, holding that hope in front of me. It was like the carrot dangling in front of the horse pulling the old milk cart, spurring him on. That belief continued to encourage me to be better, to grow, to "be ready" when Tom came home.

It did not matter to me that every circumstance, every fact, defied this possibility.

It didn't occur to me that God was healing me because he loved me or that I was growing, not for Tom, but for me, and that God was revealing himself because it's his will to do so.

As I often did when I seemed stuck and unable to go beyond my present circumstances, I'd reread *Hinds' Feet*. I always felt God underlining or highlighting a different passage in the book for closer scrutiny and clearer perception.

NOT MY WAY

I decided to go to Father Ralph's parish to sit in front of the Blessed Sacrament. I desperately needed to know if Tom was still in God's will for me.

I explained to Father Ralph, one more time, how strong my belief was, reminding him that God told me that Tom would die to self.

Father Ralph challenged me, "Andrea, God isn't saying that your marriage will be healed."

"Yes, he is," I answered confidently. "Don't you understand, Father? . . God knows me. He knows how I would interpret what he told me. He knew I would believe that Tom would come home and I do. I just can't believe anything else!"

I went into the tiny chapel, carrying my Bible and *Hinds' Feet*, desperately needing to come before God.

"I'm stuck, Lord. I must continue believing. You told me. Please help me, please . . . "

I reached for *Hinds' Feet,* leafing through it, wondering where I should begin, when my eyes fell on this passage:

"Would you be willing to trust me," he asked, "even if everything in the wide world seemed to say that I was deceiving you—indeed, that I had deceived you all along?"

She looked at him in perplexed amazement. "Why, yes," she said, "I'm sure I would, because one thing I know to be true: It is impossible that you should tell a lie. It is impossible that you should deceive me. I know that I am often very frightened at the things which you ask me to do," she added shamefacedly and apologetically, "but I could never doubt you in that way. It's myself I am afraid of, never of you, and though everyone in the world should tell me that you had deceived me, I should know it was impossible."

"O Shepherd," she implored, "don't tell me that you think I really doubt you, even when I am most afraid and cowardly and despicably weak. You know—you know I trust you. In the end I know I shall be able to say thy gentleness hath made me great."

He said nothing for a little while, only looked down very tenderly, almost pitifully at the figure now crouching at his feet. Then, after a time, he said very quietly, "Much Afraid, supposing I really did deceive you? What then?"

It was then her turn to be quite silent, trying to grasp this

NOT MY WAY

impossible thing he was suggesting and to think what her answer would be. What then?

I continued to read, my heart pounding . . .

Would it be that she could never trust, never love him again? Would she have to be alive in the world where there was no Shepherd, only a mirage and a broken lovely dream? To know that she had been deceived by one she was certain could not deceive? To lose him?

Suddenly she burst into a passion of weeping, then after a little while looked straight up into his face and said, "My Lord—if you can deceive me, you may. It can make no difference. I must love you as long as I continue to exist. I cannot live without loving you."

It was my answer . . . I knew. It was clear to me. My mind grasped the reasoning. This "deceit" that I'd believed was really the wisdom of a loving Father allowing his child to grasp a belief which gave enough hope to struggle to live. Only when he knew I was able, could he reveal the truth to me. In my pathetic "much afraid attitude," I could never have overcome my disabilities without that hope. God used my great love for Tom to heal me. In frantic desperation, I had lunged at that hope, words spoken by God years ago, capturing it like the steel jaws of a trap, unable to let it go. I could now release it.

This misunderstanding of mine had been allowed, intended. It was the only way I would have pursued this life, the reason that I struggled to become better for myself and my children. It was "The Way" that I learned about loving God and finally preferring him to Tom.

It was my gift. It was God loving me *his way*. It was my freedom, it was my life . . . I read on:

"If you can deceive me, my Lord, about the promise and the hinds' feet and the new name or anything else, you may, indeed you may, only don't let me leave you. Don't let anything turn me back."

He lifted her up, supported her by his arm, and with his own hand wiped the tears from her cheeks, then said in his strong, cheery voice, "There is no question of your turning

NOT MY WAY

back, Much Afraid. *No one, not even your own shrinking heart, can pluck you out of my hand."*

I wiped my tears from my eyes and whispered, "Thank you. Of course, you may, my Lord, you may deceive me."

I felt His presence and I felt peace. I felt courage . . . contentment. I was released from the struggle—peace enveloped me. I finally learned to love God first, then me. Now I could love unconditionally and "let go" of Tom and the outcome.

I left the chapel and Father Ralph knew by the expression on my face that I had received my answer. I shared with him my experience and together, we acknowledged that God's ways are not our ways but are so very, very far above them.

As we sat and talked about God's presence in our lives, I noticed a small relic on the fireplace. I was intrigued by it.

"What is this, Father?" I questioned as I walked over to look at it.

"It's a piece of the true Cross," he said.

I stared in disbelief at this tiny sliver of wood which held the Papal Seal on its container.

"It's authentic . . . " he said, "the cross on which Jesus was crucified."

"May I hold it?" I said.

"Of course," he responded. "You may take it with you tonight if you wish."

All night I prayed holding the container, trying to appropriately appreciate what I held in my hand. It was even more awesome to me than holding the Eucharist, for this was where it had all happened—at the Cross.

This was where Jesus had set down his life so that we could have life. The blood that he spilled on this cross healed all of us . . . restored us . . . freed us . . . Our life is in his blood.

For hours I wept and prayed, holding that cross to myself, asking God to heal and restore my brokenness.

Early the next morning when I returned to the rectory, I thanked Father for allowing me the privilege of embracing that cross. After mass I returned home, acutely aware of everything that I had experienced.

I had an eye doctor's appointment the next day and after my exam, my vision was a little blurry so I decided to drive the short distance to my mother-in-law's house to visit her.

She had been diagnosed a few months earlier with

pancreatic cancer and was extremely ill. Tom had taken a leave of absence from work to move back home with his mother to take care of her until she died. I knew how difficult this was for him but sensed that God had allowed him this privilege for a purpose.

When I arrived there, she was very, very weak. I began the usual superficial greeting and sat to talk with her. Then, as I took her hand in mine, I remembered holding the true Cross. I loved my mother-in-law very much. She had always been wonderful to all of us. I wanted so much to do something special for her.

"Mom," I said. "I'd like to pray with you if I may."

I then told her of my experience with the Cross.

She began weeping. "Andy," she said. "I must tell someone..."

She held my hand and sobbed, telling me about a tragedy that had happened to her years before that she'd carried locked in her heart. I cried with her, reminding her of the power of forgiveness, and assured her that I would take her intention to the Eucharist. I prayed with her, placing my hand, which had held the cross, on her forehead. I sensed a great relief in her.

"Thank you... thank you..." she repeated, handing over the burden that had hurt her tremendously all those years.

How incredible that God enabled me to help this woman that I loved, too.

The whole family was summoned a couple of days later. She was dying. The day after she died, Tom told his sister Pat about my visit. He had heard us sobbing and wondered what it was about. He asked Pat to call me to find out what had happened. I questioned whether it was necessary for me to tell her the details, but after praying, decided it was the right thing to do.

"I'll be right there," I said.

Tom and Pat were sitting in Mom's living room when I arrived. I shared her story with them. We all cried together. Pat said she'd always known there was unexplained pain in her mother's life. Now she had her answer. It was a gift for all of us.

When Pat left the room to get more tissues, I looked at Tom sitting in that big, familiar chair—with sadness and hurt on his wonderful face. I went to him and knelt down in front of him. I put my arms around him. I loved him, and I now knew that I loved him unconditionally. He didn't have to be mine anymore.

I apologized to him for any hurt I may have ever caused him and I asked his forgiveness. He asked for mine. We held each other and cried. We were crying for his mother . . . for ourselves . . . we cried so much we started to laugh. It was the only time in all the years that we were separated that we really connected. It was a miracle of real love.

Pat rejoined us, and as the three of us walked through the house, Tom began handing me some of his mother's religious articles, knowing I knew their value. It was his way of loving me. We laughed and laughed.

Because Mom had been so terribly ill and looked so drained in death, the family decided to have a closed casket. I offered to do her hair and makeup at the funeral parlor, reminding them that it was the last thing I could do for her. They agreed.

Later that night, the immediate family went to the funeral parlor to say their final goodbyes, and then the casket would be closed.

Tom met me at the door.

"She's beautiful, Andy. She's peaceful and looks beautiful. Thank you so much," he said, as he hugged me.

The casket remained open for all to see her radiant face.

No longer was I trudging along, dragging the weight of my desires, the carrot, the dangling hope that Tom would return, spurring me on. I had unhooked the harness that kept me bound.

"Look at me," I thought, "in spite of all I've been through . . . No, look at me *because* of all I've been through."

"Thank you, God . . . I ate the carrot!!!"

19

HAVE FUN!

It was now 1989. 1 was divorced and had just completed the annulment process. Although difficult, I was convinced that it was an appropriate closure to the legal divorce—an additional step—a spiritual process of letting go of my marriage. It was very difficult, but an extremely worthwhile endeavor, another real gift from my church. The process imparts insight and personal wisdom. And a clear understanding of what the church recognizes to be a valid, sacramental union. It required soul searching and another depth of forgiveness and acceptance. It was very worthwhile for me.

My life was full. I was very blessed with my relationship with the Lord and with all the loving, caring people who filled my life. I was not looking for more. Once again, God had a different plan.

After leading music for our First Friday Mass, I was approached by a nice looking gentleman who had some questions concerning prayer which we discussed. He asked if he could call and I said, "Of course!"

Within a few days, the phone rang and he asked, "Andrea, would you have dinner with me?"

"I'd be happy to meet with you, Richard," I responded conditionally, "*if* you want to continue our discussion about prayer."

"Well, to be totally honest with you, Andrea, I'm more interested in *you* right now than in our prayer discussion!"

I declined his invitation as gently as I could. I was not at all interested in dating.

I had been spending a lot of time in quiet prayer and

NOT MY WAY

reflection, sitting in church in the presence of the Blessed Sacrament, being still, soaking up the love and mercy of God and asking him for guidance and direction. Although I loved the more demonstrative type of prayer and worship—singing, exultation and praise—I'm equally comfortable sitting in quiet awe and reverence of this most mighty God I love.

It was in this still place one day that God spoke once again to my heart. Very clearly, I heard his words to me,

"I will be opening new doors for you, Andrea. And I want you to walk through them. I want you to have fun!"

My heart leapt at his words. Once again, a clear message from my Lord.

"I hear you, Lord. I believe this message is from you, dear God! And I'm certainly familiar with all your new doors ... but, I'm just not sure about the *'have fun'* part! I feel like I've been hanging on the cross for years. I don't understand this message."

I again prayed and asked him to clarify it for me. But once again, I felt sure that these were his words to me—*"I'll be opening new doors for you. I want you to walk through them, and I want you to have fun!"*

"Okay," I said. "If this is truly of you, Lord God, you must show me." I asked the Lord oftentimes to show me on a physical level so I'd know clearly that this is something he's asking of me.

This time I said, "A rose, dear Lord. Please, give me a rose. Place a rose in my hand and then I'll know it's of you. If you will, I will. If you don't, I won't."

My confidence and boldness comes from this most awesome, comfortable, intimate relationship of father and child ... not from a haughty place but from an honest place of truth. I cannot be obedient to his call if I'm uncertain. I must know if I'm hearing correctly, and then I can obey.

I was thrilled by this encounter; I know when the words spoken aren't mine—when he speaks. I left the church and drove home praising and thanking God ... my heart full, my spirit soaring.

When I arrived at home, my phone was ringing.

"Hi, Andrea. It's Richard."

"Oh, no!" I thought. "Not another dinner invitation." This would be the third.

"I called to invite you to dinner," he said.

NOT MY WAY

And after he spoke those words, I clearly heard another voice, *"I'm opening new doors for you and I want you to walk through them."*

I hesitated, not responding to Richard's invitation.

He immediately spoke. "Does your hesitation mean you're considering it this time? I hope it does. I realize you're probably nervous, but I assure you that you need not be fearful. Please say 'yes'. It would be *fun*! We'll *have fun*. A dinner can be *fun*."

That "fun" word rang loud in my ears. It seemed like he said it a dozen times. I could hear Richard and the Lord talking simultaneously: *"Fun . . . I want you to have fun!"*

My heart skipped. My stomach churned. I really did not want to do this. I doubted that I'd have any fun at all. I was so nervous, but I was also obedient.

"Yes," I said, slowly. "I'll go."

We made dinner arrangements and said goodbye. I became a complete basket case. "What have I done?" I bemoaned. This was an official date with a stranger and I was a wreck. "What would I say?" The worst part of it was that he was a doctor and I was only a beautician. My complete list of low self-esteem adjectives came rushing at me. I dreaded this date. How *could* this be fun? How awful!

Once again, God was asking much too much of me. This was trauma and, of course, after trying on everything in my closet, I had *nothing* to wear. This was not an evening I was looking forward to. Truly, I went only because I believed God was asking this of me . . . and even the anticipation was *not* fun.

But, I did it! Richard was a precious, gentle man and we were quite comfortable with one another. We talked a lot, sharing our love for God, who became our common ground. We both had been without our marriages for nine years and could relate to each other's experiences. We shared a lot of our beliefs and our hopes and our ideas. As our evening ended, he asked me for another date, using that "fun" word over and over, inviting me to a basketball game. I agreed and once again, we did have fun.

This time, as he brought me home, he invited me to a church dance on Valentine's Day, asking, "Do you like to dance? Wouldn't it be *fun*?" I realized that, as a physician, his extensive vocabulary included words far more sophisticated than "fun." I also knew that God was speaking this word to me over

NOT MY WAY

and over, reminding me of what he said, convincing me of his direction.

At the dance, Richard bought three raffle tickets, two for himself and one for me. We had fun dancing and really enjoyed being together. At the close of the dance, the prizes were presented. "Second prize—a beautiful, cherry table—," the chairwoman announced over the microphone, "goes to Dr. Richard Blair." How wonderful! We admired the table. This really was *fun*!

Then, drawing the final ticket, she announced the first prize. "Andrea, the first prize goes to you! It's a check for four hundred and eighty-five dollars!" I couldn't believe it! This was more than fun! This was fantastic!

Finally, she announced, "Whoever is sitting in the chair with the white sticker wins the centerpiece." A gentleman from behind me touched my shoulder and said, "You win the centerpiece, too!" Richard reached for the centerpiece and placed it in my hand.

A rose . . . ! A single rose! I was stunned!

Tears flooded my face as I looked down at my hand, remembering my ultimatum to God, "I'll do what you ask, God, but you must show me clearly. Place in my hand a rose."

My heart pounded and the tears continued to flow. Richard looked bewildered.

"I'm puzzled, Andrea," he said. "You have a check for four hundred and eighty-five dollars in one hand and I know your income is poverty level, but you're crying because you have a single rose in your other hand? I don't understand."

"I'm in his will!" I cried! "We're in his most perfect will!" Through tears of joy, I shared with Richard my prayer and its answer.

Amazingly, he had a story of his own. His third call to me was to be his final call. He had prayed, "Lord, I'd like to date this woman, but if it isn't in your most perfect will for me, I'll let it go. I feel this is the last time I'm supposed to ask her. If you want this to be, let her say 'Yes' " And, I had!

We looked at each other in wonder and in awe. And then, Richard said, "Andrea, this afternoon I ordered a dozen long-stemmed red roses to be sent to your home tomorrow."

We sat, looking at each other, acutely aware of God's touch, perhaps seeing each other for the first time. God really does know how to make *fun* happen!

NOT MY WAY

Realizing that our acquaintance was in God's will, we prayed that we remain open and willing to walk as he would have us walk, wherever that might lead us.

God, of course, never does things easily and many, many events happened in our personal lives that both hurt and blessed us. Other relationships changed. Friendships were altered. Doors opened and doors closed.

It was at this time that the Persian Gulf War threatened. The world was in turmoil. When my youngest son received orders to go to Saudi Arabia, fear once again gripped my heart. This was hard! He was my baby. I wanted to wrap him in my arms and run far, far away. This tall, strong, six-foot-four young man was still the curly, red-headed, precious baby boy I loved and wanted to protect fiercely.

My calm exterior masked the raging battle in my heart as I stood by his side at the airport as the troops were preparing for departure. Once again, I forced myself to let go of a major piece of my heart and to trust.

As the chaplain asked us to bow our heads and pray for them, I took David's hand. My silent prayer was, "Please, God, please, protect my son! Keep him safe. Return him to me."

As final goodbyes were said and people tearfully tore themselves away from the safety of each other, reporters interviewed . . . cameras flashed. Then, as he boarded the plane and the door closed, he was gone.

My day was spent praying and struggling to stay focused on the faith I had developed in God. I realized, once again, that if I was to remain hopeful and encouraging, I must place all my trust in God and stay very close to him in prayer.

The opportunities life presents causing a closer walk with God are amazing, but God always meets and reassures me in the most awesome and creative ways, extending his mercy.

That evening, I bought a newspaper. I was astonished! There, right on the front page, was a large color photograph of my son and me with our heads bowed in prayer. How unbelievable! Of all the pictures which had been taken at the airport hour after hour, this was the one on the front page! We had only prayed for a brief moment.

I felt God's merciful hand.

"It's okay," I felt him say. "I've got your son . . . I heard your prayer . . . Don't worry."

NOT MY WAY

Peace came over me. God speaks of a peace that surpasses all understanding and that's what happened. A calm assurance that David would be okay filled my mind and filled my heart. I knew that it would still be very difficult, but I believed we would get through it and he would be fine. That picture helped reassure me and my whole family.

That's the mighty God whom I serve . . . Merciful. Loving. My Father. My Protector. My Savior. My Friend. My Comforter.

Family and friends called to comment on the picture assuring me of their prayers. That photograph began a set of circumstances that only God could have initiated. Which one of the three persons of the Holy Trinity—Father, Son or Holy Spirit—has the creative genius and humor, I don't know. However, what was to happen next can only be attributed to God's creativity . . . not coincidence . . . not happenstance . . . not accident . . . but a carefully executed plan of God to bless me and encourage my growth by presenting new doors of opportunity.

The next evening, my phone rang and an unfamiliar, male voice said, "I saw your picture on the front page and was deeply moved by your face." He began sharing some personal experiences and I found myself speaking to this man about the presence and power of God in my life.

I was actively involved in an evangelization ministry in my parish, having been trained and certified by the Franciscan University of Steubenville. Recognizing one of God's unusual ways, I felt that this was the perfect opportunity to share about God and evangelize this gentleman. He asked if he could call again, explaining that he was leaving on business and would not be returning for a number of weeks but wished to speak with me again.

I agreed and thus began a long-distance ministry and interesting relationship. We seemed to share similar interests and experiences. Our main difference was in our religious beliefs, which, of course, I felt was God's main reason for this unusual encounter. God opens interesting doors.

I sent the newspaper picture to my son and prayed that my letters were encouraging and filled with hope and reassurance. Packages were sent from all of us and, although the news was dreadful, I knew to focus on God. David, being extremely talented and creative, found ways to maintain his stability. Over and over again, he'd be on the local news—he was adopted by a local preschool class and he wrote to them telling them stories about the area, about the war, and teaching them. He made the most of a terrible situation and I was so very, very proud of him. I knew God's hand was upon us all.

Weeks later, at a prayer meeting, a friend mentioned seeing our photo in the paper.

"That was quite a while ago," I commented.

"No," she said. "It was in today's morning paper." She had it with her. "The Lord must be your PR man," she said as she showed me the picture.

Once again, I looked at the picture of my son and myself, heads bowed in prayer. "This is an old picture," I said. "How strange that they would print it again! They don't usually do that!" Understanding eluded me until I arrived home.

My phone rang and again, an unfamiliar male voice spoke familiar words to me. "I saw your picture in the paper and was deeply moved by your face."

"Oh, no!" I said. At first I thought my oldest son was joking with me. He, of course, knew the story of the first gentleman and having a most incredible Irish wit would not pass up an opportunity to tease me in this manner.

However, as I listened to this gentleman, I knew it was not my son or a joke. He introduced himself and shared that he had been praying to meet a Christian woman and felt that God had inspired the call to me. I listened with interest as he shared about his wife, who had died of cancer; his two trips to Medjugorje, Yugoslavia; his children; and his impressive work in the Church. We talked for a long time, ending our conversation by agreeing to a luncheon date. Another door— "I'm walking through it, God."

I called my daughter to relate this most incredible conversation, knowing that she'd be as shocked as I. My children had witnessed some amazing "God incidences," and although they teased and kidded me a lot, they recognized God's action in all of our lives.

This was great! My daughter was now giving *me* tips on dating! She had already renamed Richard, "Doctor Dick." Now, for my luncheon date with this stranger, she was advising me to drive my own car, check out his ("Be sure to remember what kind, Mom!"), and be careful. This was *fun*!

We met and instantly liked each other. Again, our

NOT MY WAY

involvement in church and our love of God was our common denominator. We agreed on a second date which was to begin at his home where I was to tour his garden, have hors d'oeuvres, and then, we were to go to dinner.

Nothing could have prepared me for the splendor of his home—exquisite art, Waterford crystal, lavish grounds. This gentlemen was *very* wealthy . . . financially, intellectually, and spiritually. There was no way ever, in this world, that our paths would have crossed! But in God's kingdom, nothing is impossible and this was really fun! When God presents doors—choices—he doesn't necessarily make it easy. Interesting . . . awesome . . . but *not* easy.

How ironic! This rejected, uneducated beautician, barely surviving on a poverty level income, was being pursued and courted by the first caller, also wealthy—two or three nights a week, long distance; by a dedicated and gifted doctor; and by the third gentlemen, an extremely successful business man, who requested my every free evening. It was banquet time for me! God says, "I prepare a banquet for you." Well, I was partaking. All three were fine gentlemen. and, was I ever having *fun!*

What was God teaching me? To pray for wisdom in this lush time was just as important as it was in my lean time. More important, maybe, for now, man *could* provide and I needed correct discernment.

God's will was my first consideration and I needed to have real wisdom to stay focused on him. I felt that God was holding my heart and the love it contained in his hands. I, who had always walked in feelings, was being taught another way. I had to use thought and right judgment, wisdom and intelligence, for all three men were expressing their desire for continuing relationships. It was wonderful!

I did not feel unwanted, unloved and rejected anymore, but cared for and honored by these fine men. When God sets out to heal rejection, he sure knows how to do it! I had been loved and healed by my precious friends at church and in prayer group, now this! I had been learning a lot over the past nine years about love and relationships, and I felt that this was my time to walk in that wisdom. I prayed a lot and asked God to allow me to see clearly and choose well.

The first gentleman finally came home from his extended business trip and we had our first date. He arrived at my door with flowers, tall, handsome, and kind-looking. Halfway through dinner, he confessed that he had misled me about his age when he had first called and that the purpose of his lengthy business trip was to conclude his business to retire. He was five years older than he had first said and he apologized. Red flags seemed to be flying in my face. I'd asked for clarity. It was clear to me a relationship built on deceit was not for me. He'd had ample opportunity to tell me the truth earlier. He thought I was being unreasonable and harsh when I said I felt it was wise to end the relationship. Perhaps I was, but I had learned to trust myself and to recognize my needs and to validate them, to choose what was right for me, and I had. It was over.

I'd worked hard at becoming me. I had lived most of my life pleasing someone else and, as a result, had lost my identity and personhood. Now I had me and I didn't want to lose me again! I continued to date Richard and the other gentleman and continued to pray for wisdom and guidance.

One comment was impressed in my memory—their responses when they had each visited my home. Their observations were interesting to me. Richard had said, as he walked through my home, that it "reflected me—it was warm and inviting." The other commented that "I kept a nice house."

I recognized many other comments which lead me to a conclusion. Richard saw me! He had expressed a real interest in getting to know me. He even read *Hinds' Feet On High Places*, when I explained that the story, although an allegory, was one that I identified with so completely that if he wanted to understand who I was, he had only to read the book. I was very impressed when he did and shared that he, too, identified with the fears expressed in this book.

I loved his honesty and his vulnerability and his sincerity. This was a special man. He was not threatened or jealous that I was seeing someone else and not dating him exclusively but confident that God would direct us toward each other if it were to be. This "letting go" and his ability to allow me time and space to choose were most attractive. Very soon, we dated exclusively. There was real peace in my heart concerning Richard.

Peace was also being accomplished in the world. After many months of crisis, my son was coming home. On March 17th, eight very long months after his departure, I got a call.

"Hi, Mom! I'm home!" David said cheerfully. Those familiar words, which he had spoken to me since he was a little

NOT MY WAY

boy, filled my heart with joy! This was my prayed-for message from my son. He was on Manhattan Island, safe in the massive arms of Lady Liberty, having a beer, celebrating his favorite holiday, soon to be in my waiting arms.

"Happy St. Patrick's Day! Have fun, sweetheart!" I said.

"Have fun!"

NOT MY WAY

20

CROCODILE DUNDEE

My friendship with Father Ralph continued. He had prayed with and supported me through much growth and difficulty, using his profound gifts of spiritual direction and healing. He had encouraged me through my mother's death, my divorce, my awareness of sexual abuse, and now, in dating. Poor Father Ralph! I really was a challenge!

During one of our prayer sessions together, the Lord gave me an image of double iron gates. I was standing in front of them with my arms folded, barring the way. Father's discernment was that I was standing and guarding my heart. I had slammed and bolted the door and placed iron bars of protection around my wounded heart on a very deep level. He explained that if I were ever to remarry, those barriers had to come down. If I could not trust, it would not be fair to commit to an intimate relationship.

I recognized my resistance and knew that it was not God's will for me to be closed by self-protection but to be open to him and his protection, to enjoy my life to its fullest. It took me a long time to be willing to say this final "Yes," to allow my guarded heart to be vulnerable again. I was truly Much Afraid! I recognized the necessity for prayer and asked Father to arrange a weekend retreat, inviting another inner healing team to join us in prayer.

After hours of prayer, we discerned that I had erected tall and impenetrable walls which seemed to be locked from the inside. Even though I wanted my heart to be opened, it seemed hopelessly barricaded. We were all exhausted and needed a break from the intensity and the frustration we were experiencing.

We decided to stop prayer for the night, ordered a pizza, and settled in to watch a video—*Crocodile Dundee*. I was immediately captivated by the title character who carried a large knife in his belt and wore a large, black cowboy hat. I loved his looks, his mannerisms, his honesty, and I "oohed" and "aahed" my way through the whole movie. I decided that Crocodile Dundee was my ideal man. We kidded and laughed and were grateful for the lightheartedness. We decided to continue our prayer the next day and I tucked in with thoughts of Crocodile Dundee as the perfect man for me.

The next day, we began praying again. The team's discernment was that, during the time of my sexual abuse—to protect myself from the horror of what was happening—I escaped into the deepest part of my soul. I remember vowing at the time, "You can do what you want to the outside of me, but you will never get to the inside of me." How, as a child, I had that wisdom, I do not understand. But my need for that kind of protection was no longer necessary and the deepest part of my heart and soul needed to be opened to God for my wholeness.

God is a gentle man. He would never violate that locked door without my permission. Our struggle in prayer was that it was locked from the inside. I, too, was without entrance.

"Andrea, I see angels standing at the gates which guard your heart," Father said. "What's needed is your permission. Will you give your angels permission to lift you over the gates so *you* can go inside and unlock them?" After we'd been praying so hard and so long, this seemed too simple.

"Of course they can," I said, giving my permission. At that moment, I felt a release . . . a lightness . . . a lifting.

"I'm in!!!" I cried! "I'm inside my heart!" I began laughing uncontrollably. They were not sure whether I was crying or laughing, as tears poured from my eyes.

"Crocodile Dundee is in here, too!" I said laughing. "He's in my heart! It's beautiful in here! It's a lush garden with pomegranates and grapes! And a fountain! And it's wonderful! Crocodile Dundee must be the desire of my heart! He lives here! I've unlocked the doors . . . I'm free!"

The tension and serious prayer ended as we all dissolved in laughter. "Free! Free! I'm free at last!" I cried! "Free to love again!"

It was Alleluia time! God truly does set the captives free, whether the imprisonment is of one's own making or someone else's. It can be overcome. Yeah, God! I was very grateful to Father Ralph and the prayer team. What a mighty God we serve!

Soon after this incredible prayer experience, a group of

NOT MY WAY

us planned a second trip to Medjugorje, Yugoslavia, where the Blessed Mother was appearing to young people. She was calling the world to prayer. Pilgrims came, from all over the world, to partake of the holiness, healings, and visions.

I felt that God was directing me to go to Medjugorje to experience the gentle touch of Mother Mary and to listen to the witness of the children she was appearing to. I knew it was Mary's role to lead all to her son Jesus to repent of our sinful and careless ways and to pray for world peace and reconciliation with God. I also knew it was God's will for me to go, for once again he provided the way—a ticket purchased for me by a dear friend who believed I was to go.

My relationship with the blessed virgin Mary was weak. I'd grown to understand real relationship with her son Jesus, therefore I had a basis for comparison. How and why I could not feel a closeness to Mary as my Mother bothered me. My prayers to her came from my head, not my heart, and I was very aware of the difference.

I knew God was my Father. I'd experienced Jesus as my Lord, my Savior, my friend and brother. I walk in the empowerment of the Holy Spirit. Why not Mary? After years of questioning and struggling, I finally understood. My own precious mother, in her subservience to my wonderful dad, had unknowingly denied me the true gift of a strong relationship with herself as a separate personality. Only after Dad's death were we truly focused on one another. In my loving Tom I'd also deferred to his stronger personality. How easily our patterning and programming happens.

I believe many people defer to the stronger personality thereby neglecting to bring the correct balance of healthy relationships to one another and to our children. Therefore identity with one parent gets weakened and a loss is experienced. I had not felt the necessity to pursue my relationship with Mary, she was just there. When I really began to question, I better understood God's perfect plan.

He did not call us into being through a stone or a grain of sand but formed us in our mothers' wombs. Both father and mother are vital in creation, equal . . . God's plan! Honor thy Father and thy Mother . . . God's plan. Equally yoked . . . Gods plan. He created for our patterning the perfect holy family—mother and father responsible for God's own son . . . God's plan!

NOT MY WAY

It was God's plan that Mary be conceived without sin which established her as the only suitable and fitting spouse for his Holy Spirit, the only pure and virginal chalice to contain his son. Because of God's grace Mary was free from dysfunctional and distorted patterning. Her "Yes" to God was freely given. She was not influenced by guilt, manipulation, fear or any sinful attitude. She was healthy and whole. Only when you possess your own will can you freely give it.

At the foot of the cross Mary bore the weight of her pain with dignity, also forgiving those who killed her child and once again accepting God's will as he spoke his last words to her. "Woman, there is your son" and then to the apostle John, "There is your mother." God identified for us all the relationship he was giving us with Mary.

I had shared with a priest my concerns, and his insights gave me the key to understanding.

He asked, "Do you have any children?"

When my response was yes he continued, "Do you have a daughter . . . ?"

My eyes filled with tears as my heart felt the great love I have for her. "Yes, I have a wonderful daughter," I responded.

A mother can wait for years before her children really recognize their incredible love and come to her with open arms and heart. I understood!

"Oh, Mary," I cried . . . "How long have you waited for me?" How excellent to have a perfect pattern. She became one with the Spirit, brought forth the Son and desired to do God's will . . . My desire is to grow up to be just like my Mom . . .

This trip was an extraordinary blessing for me.

One afternoon, Father Ralph and I took a walk through the sprawling vineyards that had already been picked clean for harvest. We both stopped abruptly, as together we faced a double iron gate, just like the one I'd envisioned in prayer a few weeks before.

"Open it and walk in, " Father said.

My heart pounded as I lifted the latch. Both gates were unlocked. I stepped inside the vineyard and hanging just inside the gate, full and ripe, was one, last lush cluster of grapes.

"Take them," Father Ralph said. "Partake of their fruit. I'm sure God left them there just for you."

As I plucked them and held them in my hand, the owner of the vineyard appeared.

NOT MY WAY

"Come! Taste! I have new wine!" he said. "Come! Taste! Drink! Please, drink!"

We did. The promise of new life, lush and full, was the message I received from God. Pomegranate trees grew there. I was in the garden of my heart . . . free to open and close the door. Once again, God manifested, on a physical realm, his closeness to me.

We climbed Mount Krishevec and from its peak, we could see the valley below. I knew I had reached another plateau like Much Afraid. I had my hinds' feet and I could run and leap with freedom! I had my new name, "Glory," and grace for a new beginning. I looked forward to real, new possibilities in my life. I did not feel fear but a sense of anticipation. Life seemed fuller and more fun, and I was deeply grateful to God for the new life he was giving me.

The morning after I returned home, in my gratitude and prayer, I said, "Dear Lord, what would you have me do in this new life you have given me? I come to do your will. My desire is to please you . . . "

"My child, you will please me if you live your life. Not as I or someone else would choose for you, but your choice. You are in a state of unrest and displeasure because you are never quite sure how you are to choose. My child, try to choose. I will lead you if the choices are wrong. But if you do not choose or move, how can I lead? You will always wait for someone's direction, someone's suggestion as to how and what you are to do. Decide for yourself what you would like to do."

For the first time in my life, I understood that it was *my* life. I did please God and he wanted *me* to please *me*. We agreed. He wanted me to choose. He gave me the freedom to choose—not just to be obedient—but to make decisions.

I was still seeing Richard and growing in my appreciation of him. He was patient and kind. He was slow to anger. He was not jealous. He was—as Scripture describes in *1 Corinthians*: 13: 4-7—love. I was honored and respected. There was such freedom in the unconditional acceptance that he gave me. Only God can initiate this type of love. My heart was opening, and the precious heart that it embraced was Richard's.

One morning, in prayer, I said to God, "Father, if I were to ever remarry, who would it be? I know I'm your precious daughter, the daughter of the Most High God. Who would You have me marry?"

NOT MY WAY

"My beloved son," he responded.

"Of course," I said. "That makes sense. You would not have me unequally yoked. Of course, it would be to your son."

Later that day, Richard called. "Andrea, would you like to go to Friendly's for ice cream?"

"Sure!" I said.

As we were eating ice cream, I remembered my encounter in prayer that morning. Looking at Richard, I said thoughtfully . . . "Who are you?"

"I'm . . . um . . . " he thought for a moment, as he spooned ice cream in his mouth. "I'm the beloved son of the Father," he said with assurance.

My "Holy Spirit chills" rippled through me, as I looked into his deep blue eyes. My daughter would have sung "Do do do do . . . .do do do do!"—the theme from the Twilight Zone.

Clear? Yes! I'm walking, Lord! I'm choosing! I'm having fun!

One day, Richard invited me to drive with him to visit his son in college. We would spend the day, shop, have dinner, and return home. I agreed. It sounded like it would be lots of fun. As we were driving, I glanced at Richard and as I looked at his handsome face, I felt a tug at my heart and a stirring deep within me and for one brief moment, God allowed me to see his heart. It was beautiful and gentle, sweet and pure. Tears filled my eyes as I looked at him. God allowed me this little peek into the preciousness of this very special man. My heart warmed and I praised God.

Later, as we were shopping, we were being silly and I found some hats in the men's department and asked Richard to try them on. He agreed and we laughed as he modeled one after the other. He tried on a big, black cowboy hat and turned from the mirror toward me, with a grin on his face.

My heart stopped. My eyes opened wide.

"Crocodile!" I thought to myself. "*He's* Crocodile Dundee!" I thought my heart would burst. He's my ideal man. *Richard* . . . he's the desire of my heart.

Soon after, on my birthday, on our knees in prayer Richard asked me to become his wife. My answer was, of course, "Yes!" I had my Crocodile Dundee, the beloved son of the Father, my ideal man. We knew that we would be one in heart. We knew God was doing the joining. Our "Yes" was our "Amen" to God.

NOT MY WAY

I called my daughter and through laughter and tears, told her I was engaged. This most beautiful and precious young woman had struggled for years loving me, knowing in her own broken heart, my pain. Now she shared my joy!

The very next morning she and I went shopping for a wedding gown. One after another, I tried them on.

"Oh, Mom," she gasped as she zipped up one of the gowns. "Look! "

I stepped in front of the mirror.

"It's perfect! Never mind the price!" she said.

It was white, expressing the purity of love I felt for Richard. I bought it!

One evening, Richard and I were having dinner and discussing wedding plans when he changed the subject. He told me about a check he had received from a doctor he knew. The heading on the check bothered him. The doctor had put his name first, along with the letters depicting his credentials and degree above his wife's name. She had no titles, no credentials, and Richard felt it looked demeaning.

I kidded with him and said, "Not to worry, sweetheart! We can put my name and my title first on our checks."

"What title, darling? You don't have one."

"Oh, yes I do!" I said, smiling mischievously. "D.M.H.G.!" .

"What's D.M.H.G.?" Richard asked, with a puzzled expression on his face.

"Sweetheart," I said. "it's taken me years to know who I am—my true identity as God's child. I am . . . *Daughter of the Most High God*. He's my Master and Educator. I'm entitled to that title."

He smiled lovingly at me and said, "You sure are." After our marriage, he ordered our checks exactly that way with my name and title first, then his!

We continued to make plans for a November wedding and could hardly wait. We decided to be married with a large church celebration that included all our family and friends.

I was given two wedding showers. The prayer team, who had prayed me into my heart, smiled knowingly as they handed me three numbered packages to be opened in order. The first, a huge knife; the second, a video; and the third, a very large black hat with crocodile teeth.

Richard, my handsome "Crocodile Dundee," grinned,

NOT MY WAY

placed the hat on his head, took me in his arms, and kissed me. All our guests laughed and cheered!

All of our children were in our wedding. My beautiful daughter was maid of honor and Richard's handsome son, his best man. Our daughters wore white, including my daughter-in-law who was pregnant, full of the new life growing within her, who was to be our first granddaughter. Our sons wore black, with purple, depicting the royalty we felt as children of the Most High God.

The music at our wedding was the gift from the ecumenical choir I sang with, which presented Christian concerts, and the entire choir sang our magnificent Nuptial Mass. Our's was a true celebration. Four priests and one deacon, our very dear friends, said mass. I walked alone down the aisle to the song, "Glory to the King." I looked like royalty and I was—Daughter of the Most High God. I knew Father-God was giving me to his beloved son.

After our lovely reception, when we arrived at the hotel, Richard unlocked the door to our room and said, "Wait here, sweetheart." One moment later, he appeared with his Crocodile Dundee hat, grinned, swooped me up into his arms, and carried me over the threshold into our room. I knew I liked his style.

Crocodile Dundee was definitely for me!

NOT MY WAY

21

MY PRECIOUS JEWELS

During the last fifteen years, Holy Scripture has been a tremendous blessing to me. It has guided, directed, consoled and enlightened me. It has given me encouragement and strength when I've been without hope and in despair. It has caused me to reflect and to ponder opening my mind to embrace God's revelation of himself to me. It has taught me much about myself. God's word is living and applicable to every circumstance that presents itself. It is conversation with God. It is his Word. It is his letter of love to all of us and our instruction book.

Scripture is the most powerful construction tool for tearing down barriers and rebuilding lives available to man... it moves mountains. It also speaks in a whisper, sometimes barely audible until one really listens. Scripture is like fine wine, not to be gulped but tasted, savored. Each taste reveals more clearly its contents until its fruits are recognized.

There is a passage in the Bible that has given me much cause for reflection. When I first read it I knew I needed to reread it—to mull it around the taste buds of my mind. This Scripture in St. Paul's letter to the Ephesians is about loving. In Chapter 5, verse 28, it says "That is how husbands should treat their wives, loving them as parts of themselves. For since a man and his wife are now one—a man is really doing himself a favor and loving himself when he loves his wife. No one hates his own body, but lovingly cares for it, just as Christ cares for his body the church, of which we are all parts."

As I read this about loving and hating one's own body, I thought about Tom's cancer. Can one love one's own body when that body is riddled with cancer, threatening to take your life—when you are robbed of health and vigor and joy? Are you betrayed? Does your own body become a prison? How great is the need to escape it? Does logic and love get buried someplace under the enormous weight of uncertainty and fear?

Could this be part of the answer to my question—what happed to my marriage? Can these few lines of Scripture be the answer to years of wondering why? How could Tom love me if

NOT MY WAY

I were part of that body. That thought brought peace to my questioning heart. It consoled me.

I have also learned over the past fifteen years that God either initiates or allows the circumstances in our lives. He says in Holy Scripture in Isaiah 55:9: *"This plan of mine is not what you would work out. Neither are my thoughts the same as yours. For just as the heavens are higher than the earth, so are my ways higher than yours. And my thoughts higher than yours."*

His ways are above our ways. Unfathomable sometimes, completely outside our capacity to grasp and comprehend. We question, "If you really loved me, how could you allow this, God?" My intellect and I have gone round and round ... "You can't allow this," or "Why, it isn't right," or "It makes no sense," or "How can this be?" Over and over in my personal life and in the lives of those around me and in the world, I've asked "Why?"

A few things I've learned have helped stop my demanding questions. I don't need to have answers—God's ways *are* above my ways. I've learned that I cannot properly perceive an event or a specific set of circumstances since the final outcome has not yet been revealed and I'm seeing only a small fragment of the whole picture.

The greatest and most profound truth that I've learned is that most of the things that we blame God for are often our own doing. We are not his robots, programmed to obey. We are his children, given choices to make as we will. The end result, the manifestation and consequences of some of those choices have been disastrous for all of mankind. God has given us dominion over all things. That's scary!

Our freedom to choose is an awesome responsibility. We don't understand the power that is in our hands. That freedom is like presenting a child with a live hand grenade to play with. The outcome could be disastrous.

God does involve himself in our lives, though, in a tremendously personal and intimate way and can turn all the circumstances to good. I'm living proof of that!

I've learned that the relationships that have been given in my life are gifts to me. They are as precious as jewels. I believe each one is allowed by God. He's presented me with priceless jewels—my friends. They make me more beautiful. I believe they're hand picked ... of rare quality ... priceless.

NOT MY WAY

They are the men and women whose lives have touched mine. They have taught, influenced, loved, healed, and restored me. The lessons have not all been pleasant, and sometimes the relationships have been difficult.

Faces come to mind and tears blur my vision, and I thank God for each and every one of them. My gratitude for each one is beyond my vocabulary. The love held in my heart for each will always remain.

As I reflect on all my blessings, I reach for my Bible. It opens to *Isaiah 54*. The pages are worn, underlined and taped. I've touched them as often as they've touched me. This particular scripture was given to me years ago by a friend who felt inspired to share it with me. Back then the passage served as a comfort and a blessing, reminding me that the Lord, my Maker, was my husband. Now, I'm able to comprehend the enormity of its message, for it has all been realized. It's truth to me.

Sing, oh childless woman. Break out into loud and joyful song, Jerusalem. For she who was abandoned has more blessings now than she whose husband stayed. Enlarge your house, build on additions, spread out your home for you will soon be bursting at the seams! And your descendants will possess the cities left behind during the exile, and rule the nations that took their lands.

Fear not; you will no longer live in shame. The shame of your youth and the sorrows of widowhood will be remembered no more, for your Creator will be your "husband." The Lord of hosts is his name; he is your Redeemer, the Holy One of Israel, the God of all the earth. For the Lord has called you back from your grief—a young wife abandoned by her husband.

For a brief moment, I abandoned you. But with great compassion I will gather you. In a moment of anger I turned my face a little while; but with everlasting love I will have pity on you, says the Lord your Redeemer. Just as in the time of Noah, I swore that I would never again permit the waters of a flood to cover the earth and destroy its life, so now I swear that I will never again pour out my anger on you as I have during this exile. For the mountains may depart and the hills disappear, but my kindness shall not leave you. My promise of peace for you will never be broken, says the Lord who has mercy upon you.

NOT MY WAY

O my afflicted people, tempest tossed and troubled, I will rebuild you on a foundation of sapphires and make the walls of your houses from precious jewels. I will make your towers of sparkling agate, and your gates and walls of shining gems. And all your citizens shall be taught by me, and their prosperity shall be great. You will live under a government that is just and fair. Your enemies will stay far away; you will live in peace. Terror shall not come near. If any nation comes to fight you, it will not be sent by me to punish you. Therefore, it will be routed, for I am on your side.

I have created the smith who blows the coals beneath the forge and makes the weapons of destruction. And I have created the armies that destroy. But in that coming day, no weapon turned against you shall succeed, and you will have justice against every courtroom lie. This is the heritage of the servants of the Lord. This is the blessing I have given you, says the Lord.

I have learned to "sing" because of my circumstances; to praise God for all things. I do have more blessings—my self, my Richard, his two children, and his brother—because of my abandonment.

I no longer live in the shame of my youth—the abuse but glory in the victory of it.

His kindness will never leave me, and the intimacy I've experienced with him is likened to a loving husband . . . I know I'm the bride of Christ.

I experience the peace of the *23rd Psalm* in my lovely "enlarged" house with Richard. I have been rebuilt on a new foundation; the rock of my salvation is Jesus Christ.

I have received precious stones, just as Much Afraid received them, validating my efforts of self-sacrifice, having been "born again," created anew through the power of Christ.

I witness the teachings of my family and friends by my Lord and see them prosper in his truths. I live with the unconditional love of Richard, experiencing its freedom. He is on my side. I will remain by his side.

God manifested another reminder for me, another assurance of the *rightness* of my marriage to Richard, and, as usual, it was manifested in the physical realm

When Richard and I married, we received many lovely gifts—fine and beautiful, gifts that the world provides. But I

NOT MY WAY

received a gift from a special friend that I will always treasure. Because of our friendship, she knew of my relationship with the book, *Hinds' Feet on High Places*. She knew my life and how I had gathered little stones—little pebbles—to remind myself, as Much Afraid did, of the different healings I'd experienced, the struggles, and the attitudes I'd set down.

This special gift was wrapped in beautiful paper, tied with ribbons with a real rose: a little velvet pouch. I opened the pouch and emptied the contents in my hand. I gasped. They were beautiful, multi-colored stones that resembled precious jewels—ruby red, emerald green, clear, pearl, blue. This gift was from her caring heart. I will always treasure it. We share its meaning. Not only did they symbolize Much Afraid's precious jewels but also the shining gems in the chapter from *Isaiah*.

When Richard and I moved to our new home, I lovingly placed them on my kitchen counter and put behind them a simple statue of a woman kneeling in prayer. Her humble posture of acceptance and desire continues to remind me of who I am and where I've come from.

One day, I was talking on the phone with a dear friend as I picked up the stones and was cleaning the counter. I told her what I was doing. She jokingly asked, "Which one of those stones is me?"

I said, "Oh, I don't know. Why?"

"Do you have a little one?" she queried.

"Yeah, I do. It's green and it's little."

"I want to be that stone," she said kiddingly.

I said, "Okay. I'll name that stone after you."

Then, as I held them in my hands, I knew that they represented not just the circumstances or the healing, but the people God used for my lessons and blessings.

"Oh!" I said with delight. "I can name them all."

There was a bright green one that I named after my Irish priest, Father Ralph. A red one—Father Regis, filled with the Holy Spirit. A honey-brown one that reminded me of the warm, soothing eyes of a friend whom I will always cherish and love. A jagged one reminded me of a relationship that cut and wounded and hurt but taught me so much. Three pearlescent stones—dear and loyal friends. Three beautiful blue stones—my mother, my grandmother, and my favorite aunt. A many-faceted stone that I named "Richard" because of the depth

NOT MY WAY

and beauty that he has brought into my life. There are so many other stones, all identified and treasured by me. I love each one.

For Christmas three years ago, my oldest son, Tom, presented me with a little box and I opened it.

"Merry Christmas, Mom!" The small box contained three more stones.

"This first one, the gray one," he explained, "is me!"

I'm sure he didn't realize it, but this small stone was shaped like the Rock of Gibraltar. "It *is* him," I thought to myself, "showing his strength of character. He's honorable, loving, dependable, and responsible. He's faithful, capable, and full of Irish wit."

"The second stone is Kathy," Tom continued. I thought of his beautiful wife, warm, caring, and gentle.

"And the third one is for Caitlyn," he concluded. Tears of gratitude blurred my vision as I gazed at the tiny stone, a tiny pink stone, representing his precious daughter—my first grandchild, Caitlyn. Tom and Kathy now have another precious daughter, Sara Anne... I've added a tiny pearl for her.

My youngest son's stone is Irish green. Justice and kindness are his attributes. David is gifted and talented, tender, creative, and loyal. He has passion, humor, and love.

Two more small, pink stones were added by his wonderful stepdaughter, Heather, who said, "Here, Grandma, these can be Mom and me." The warm, generous, and loving personalities of my daughter-in-law, Wendy, and Heather, my granddaughter, have blessed us all. I added another tiny green stone—David and Wendy's darling baby girl, Taylor. We are now thrilled to add a tiny brilliant blue stone for our first grandson, Connor James, David and Wendy's latest blessing.

My daughter, Kelly, a most beautiful jewel, sparkles with goodness. Her great gift is in giving. She radiates love, kindness, and compassion and unselfishly shares her talents and time, blessing all who encounter her. Her stone sits on my counter with all the others as she is being formed by God—cut and polished—so that she becomes her most beautiful. She's a diamond.

Two more valuable, multicolored stones from God's most generous hand are my two wonderful stepchildren—Rick and Jolene. They're adventurous, bright, caring, and accepting like their dad.

I've added others—vibrant and beautiful—for new

NOT MY WAY

friends who have moved into my heart, reminding me of God's gifts. The personalities, the relationships that are woven into the tapestry of my life are placed there for a purpose.

Nothing is an accident; nothing is a coincidence.

When you've given your life to God, and he becomes the jeweler of that life, he cuts and polishes and creates the priceless crown that we are to wear into eternity.

He's the most precious jewel of all.

NOT MY WAY

22

HIS MOST HOLY LAND

Richard and I planned a trip to the Holy Land. Our pilgrimage was to be with the Franciscan University in Steubenville, Ohio, where I'd received my training for evangelization. I had attended many conferences for youth and leadership at the spirit-filled charismatic university where Christ's message is not only taught but lived. I knew that the tour of the Holy Land would be a rich, spiritual adventure with them. We would be touring, sight-seeing, studying, and celebrating daily mass. What a privilege to walk where Jesus walked—to experience the places, the sights, the wonders of Jerusalem, Bethlehem, Nazareth, Cana—all the awesome, wondrous places we've read about in Scripture.

However, upon our arrival in the Holy Land, I was sick. I was experiencing two extremely unpleasant ailments and I felt awful. I was irritated, upset, and distracted, focusing on my physical condition and missing some of the blessings. I questioned, in an annoyed and exasperated tone, "Why here, Lord? Why now? I came all this way. I'm here in your Holy Land on a bus with a tour. This is *not* where I want to be sick. I'm never sick. What's going on? This is not the time or the place for laryngitis and diarrhea."

However, like it or not, I was sick. I fought with myself to arrive at a place of peace and acceptance, realizing there was little I could do to change the circumstances. I prayed a lot, knowing that God could use this unpleasantness to teach me if I remained open.

I began to really listen. I'm afraid sometimes laryngitis is the only answer to closing my mouth and opening my ears. I also prayed that if I was really being emptied, physically, that I become acutely aware of what still needed to "go" in my life to make more room for God. I'd learned to think this way. It's the Serenity Prayer in action: *"Lord, grant me the ability to accept*

NOT MY WAY

the things I cannot change; to change the things I can; and the wisdom to know the difference."

It's wisdom to think like that. It's a green light of permission for God to turn, as Scripture promises, all circumstances into good. The prayer says, "Yes, I desire to be more like you. Whatever habit or sin disables and hinders me, I'd like it to go. I'd like to be cleansed of it. I'd like to be filled with you, Lord." That was my prayer.

As we traveled through this wondrous Holy Land, visiting places I'd only read about, the stories in Scripture became alive and real. We renewed our baptismal vows in the Jordan River. We experienced the desert of John the Baptist. We walked the *Via Dolorosa,* carrying the cross and experienced what we expect was similar to the reality of the sacred walk that Jesus took. On-lookers were indifferent, shopkeepers were selling things. Others were laughing and joking, looking at us, wondering what we were so solemn about, wondering why we were crying as each of us took a turn bearing the weight of the cross.

We stood praying in the Upper Room, acutely aware of the miracle of the first Pentecost, when the promised Spirit of Jesus filled his disciples, enabling and empowering them to carry out their mission of spreading the Gospel. What a wondrous and glorious trip we were having!

We were learning a lot more about Jewish laws, customs, and tradition, too. I learned how great and profound the changes were that Jesus' presence required of his people: a totally new concept of how to live—new rules, new laws, new ways, a new language, all so foreign to their familiar understanding. New ways require setting down old ways, putting to death concepts that no longer apply. Our Jewish guide and the priests and scholars we traveled with taught us as we visited each place.

My mind kept focusing on the mercy of Jesus. I was understanding his compassion and his ability to freely love those who came to him unconditionally. Stories from Scripture became more and more alive as I walked this holy ground—the blind man, the leper, the demon-possessed man, whose only hope was Jesus. How incredible their courage and faith must have been as they approached him, recognizing him to be their only answer for healing and hope.

I thought a lot about the story of the woman caught in

adultery and meditated on Jesus' knowledge, understanding, and patience. Both she and her accusers were allowed to examine themselves and repent of their sins privately. He protected them even from the revelation of his gaze as he looked down at the ground. No stones were hurled to kill. What incredible mercy! What profound understanding of humanity!

I was also learning more about guilt . . . judgments. I was forced to really listen because I was too uncomfortable to speak. My hearing improved as did my thinking! How quickly I can offer a judgment . . . find someone lacking or guilty. How often do I really look at myself before I hurl my stones of criticism? How often am I willing to divert my gaze to allow recovery from sin and mistake? Or am I there, ready to expose it in my self-righteousness? How loving is that? I felt so convicted. I felt remorse and guilt, bearing the weight of my sin. My self loomed large and loud . . . clanging in my ears, without love, a noisy gong, a clanging cymbal. That's how I sound when mercy and love and compassion are forgotten. How easy to retaliate to circumstances in ways that destroy.

Where is my mercy? Where is my compassion?

My heart was heavy. I cried quietly . . . silently . . . grateful for the silence that enabled me to really hear. Grateful for my laryngitis . . . understanding how accurate the diarrhea was. "Thank you for purification and for your revelation, Lord. I did need to be emptied of a lot." In humility and with a contrite heart, I went to confession. I thanked God for speaking so clearly to me. I accepted my illness and my discomfort.

The next day, we were to go to Mount Tabor, the top of the mountain known as the Mount of Transfiguration, where Jesus revealed his glory to John and James, where he was transfigured before them. I still felt quite ill, drained both physically and emotionally. I needed to find a place to rest.

In the courtyard near the top of Mount Tabor, I saw a very old bench made of poured concrete which encircled a tree in front of the cathedral. "Thank you, Lord!" I said. Turning to Richard, I told him, "I'll sit on that bench over there and wait for the rest of you. It looks like the only place to sit down!"

I walked to the bench and before sitting, I looked down. I could not believe my eyes. Drawn in the cement was a symbol of the Crusader's Cross. Under the cross, one name alone was printed, embedded in the cement, "Andrea." No other name . . . just mine. No other drawings.

NOT MY WAY

My gasp and my cry alerted those around me that something extraordinary was happening. As they looked at the bench, very little had to be explained. My name and the cross said it all. Tears of joy flooded my face . . . indescribable joy filled my heart.

My awe must have matched that of James and John as I, too, witnessed the glory of God on Mount Tabor. The awareness of his mercy reached my soul, and I felt the magnitude of his love. He knew I would need a place to sit. He drew me there. How many, many years before was my name written in the concrete of the old bench? How excited God must have been watching me walk to that spot, knowing I would see my gift and see him.

The extent of his kindness, I will never comprehend. Joy and ecstasy filled my being. "My God, my God, this sacred place, this holy mountain, my name." I made it to the top! I was in the kingdom of love with my Savior. Much Afraid had her hinds' feet. I had mine, too! I was there at the top of the mountain. I, too, was filled with Grace and Glory; I, too, a crusader. How can one experience such heavenly grandeur on a human level? I was in such a special place, so aware of God's love for me.

The next day, we were scheduled to visit a gift shop that had been suggested by our tour director. The owner of the shop explained about some of the articles, suggesting an appropriate purchase of remembrance of our visit would be the Crusader's Cross. Because it was our third wedding anniversary, Richard decided to purchase one for me. I shared with the owner, a Palestinian Christian, my incredible experience on Mount Tabor. His eyes filled with tears as he said he, too, had experienced the mercies of Jesus. He told Richard that he would personally make a special cross just for me and deliver it to our hotel the next evening.

"Trust me," he said. "I will make it just for you. Trust me." He and Richard agreed on the price and we did as he asked, trusting him to design it.

The following evening, he met us in our hotel lobby. I opened the box with shaking hands and beheld the Crusader's Cross, a magnificent work of art. I cried so hard I could hardly see it! He had fashioned it in solid gold and had placed within the cross five diamonds, representing the five wounds Christ

NOT MY WAY

suffered at the crucifixion. I continued to cry as he explained about the perfection of the diamonds.

I was remembering Much Afraid and her agonizing climb to the top of the mountain as well as God's promise that when she overcame her crooked mouth and her crippled ways, he would turn the worthless little stones that she gathered into precious jewels. She would be transformed from poor, pathetic, crippled little Much Afraid and he would change her name to "Grace and Glory." It was on Mount Tabor where Christ revealed his glory. It was there, on the top of Mount Tabor, where I read my name. It was all too wondrous for me to believe.

Through my tears, I did my best to explain to him my story. We all cried and shared in the magnificent love and mercy of Our Lord and Savior, Jesus Christ, revealed to us once again in his most Holy Land.

It had been a most incredible trip and our last day in the Holy Land finally arrived. My only disappointment was that I had not been able to keep a promise to David, my younger son, who is a policeman.

He collects police patches, and whenever we travel, he gives some to me to trade with officers in other parts of the world. On this trip, however, because we traveled on a tour bus, we were not free to explore unscheduled places and had been unable to locate a police station.

"Please, Lord," I pleaded for David. "Just one little patch."

We were to drive to Bethlehem, celebrate mass in the church at the site where Jesus was born, and then travel back to Jerusalem to visit the Upper Room. We then would go immediately to the airport to fly to Rome for the last third of our phenomenal trip.

When I stepped off the bus in Bethlehem, I couldn't believe my eyes. We were parked next to a police station.

"Oh, Richard, hurry!" I said, as I ran to its entrance.

I was stopped abruptly by two policemen with machine guns. That didn't stop me! I was so thrilled and excited that I had found a police station, I wasn't afraid. God had provided again. I attempted to explain to them, in my exuberance, that I wanted to trade a patch but was getting a very strong negative response from them. Undaunted, I continued to plead with them.

NOT MY WAY

"No! No! No!" they said as they stubbornly shook their heads.

"Please," I continued. "For my son . . . "

Finally, one of them scowled, took the patch, and walked stridently into the police station.

I closed my eyes tightly and said, "Oh, Lord, please!"

He returned a moment later, and I held out my open hand. It was not a patch, but a hat clip. It was the Star of David! How extraordinary as I threw my arms around each of the policemen with their machine guns. "Thank you! God bless you!" I said.

How perfect for my David . . . the Star of David in Bethlehem.

"Thank You, God." I prayed, clutching the Star of David as we ran into the church. We were late and our tour guide hurriedly motioned to us, directing us.

In utter amazement, I dropped to my knees. Painted on the floor, at the very site of Christ's birth, was a magnificent Star of David.

I placed the Star of David in my hand on the Star of David where Christ was born. I wept as I touched that holy place. I prayed for my son. For all my children. For their children. And for all the generations to come.

We were all profoundly touched by holiness in his most holy land.

23

THE HIGH PLACES

It was exciting to be Richard's wife. We decided to sell each of our homes and buy a new home that would be *ours*. Now, this was *really fun*! I knew that when I met our realtor. She was special and believed she'd find the right house for us, which she did. When I stepped into the foyer, we both knew. It felt perfect to me!

She said as she smiled at me, "You look like you belong in this house." I realize that's a well-used realtor's line, but I *did* look like I belonged in this house with its serenity and beauty that was more than structural.

When we walked outside and I saw its number—23—I knew for sure. Richard and I loved the *23rd Psalm*. We had received a framed print as a wedding gift and believed God led us to this house, where we were to live with our Shepherd.

Our new home was large and beautiful, high above the city in a lovely, wooded area. I just couldn't get over how lovely it was . . . and how large! I smiled as I remembered God's word in *Isaiah* about "enlarging your tent!" Never in a million years had I ever expected to live in such an elegant home!

We had moved about an hour away from family and friends to be close to Richard's work. We lived in the land of garage door openers, where the single touch of a button can isolate you from friendly interaction with neighbors. I began to feel lonely.

I had been very busy with all the activity necessary for settling us into this beautiful new home—now it was done! Richard's work was very time consuming and I had very little left to do. I began to miss my family, my friends, and my church activities. I had been so involved in work and ministry; now, time seemed to be what I had the most of.

I especially missed music ministry, my favorite expression of prayer. I loved singing and playing the violin and leading praise. I would listen for the direction of the Spirit,

NOT MY WAY

pray aloud, and lead the singing during quiet worship and adoration. It was a wonderful gift. I felt very close to God at these times.

One of my favorite responsibilities, however, was playing the maracas during the liveliest songs of praise, maintaining the rhythm which encouraged the spirit of joy, guiding the assembly to celebration and prayer.

Now, schedules in our new life conflicted with my being able to return to participate in music ministry. I understood the difficulty of my dearest friends in the music ministry and their frustration with an absent praise leader. I found it impossible to let go of this ministry completely, requesting a temporary leave of absence, believing that in three or four months I'd be available to continue to lead the praise and worship at the First Friday Masses. I was being asked to pray about letting it go completely, and this wasn't easy. To let go would cut the final tie to all that had so blessed and nurtured me—my dear, dear friends; my community at church; and the usefulness I felt ministering for God. I loved playing the maracas and praising! This is going to take a lot of prayer.

In our new community, Richard and I joined a large, Catholic Church, whose pastor was an inspiring, holy priest and whose associate pastors we liked very much. It didn't quite feel like home, though; I felt disconnected. My former church, which had become my extended family whom I missed very much, still seemed to draw me back.

Now, I was faced with a decision—what would be God's will in this instance? My will, of course, would be to keep what I had—comfort and a feeling of usefulness. Would God's will be to let it go, to set it down? I feared this because of my new circumstances.

I wanted my usual clear message from God, so I put off asking him, rationalizing that I really wouldn't have to do it if I didn't ask.

The day eventually came when I felt that I'd better pray since the music ministry had been waiting for my decision long enough. One of my new neighbors, a Christian lady from the Presbyterian Church who had welcomed me when we first moved into the area, had recommended a wonderful book for me to read and offered to loan me hers—dropping it in my mailbox a few weeks previously.

As I sat to pray, I remembered this book and decided to

NOT MY WAY

glance through it before I began any serious prayer about music ministry. I opened it and stared in disbelief. My eyes focused on a picture of a woman—clearly disturbed, scowling, jaw set, the cords in her neck tight, straining. Her expression was rigid and stern, and clutched tightly in her hands were maracas! The caption describing the picture was "Let Go!!!"

Tears stung my eyes as I shook my head: first, "no" in disbelief; then, "yes" in surrender. My emotions were mixed as they usually were when God spoke so clearly to me—sadness and fear to give up my ministry and let go . . . gratitude for his presence . . . awe of his faithfulness. "Thank You, Lord," I prayed, as I figuratively pried my fingers off of my maracas and graciously set them down.

For many years, since 1983, I believed that God was telling me to write, to share some of his marvelous deeds. Over and over I would get this message and I did write, privately. I kept journals and wrote of inspirations I felt were from him with the understanding that he wanted his deeds recorded and shared in ways beyond my personal testimony to individuals and small groups. The word "write" became more than an instruction just for my own personal growth, but I was to share my writings with others.

Once again, though, my old inadequacies and low self-esteem became larger than my faith. Because I had no college education—no degree in anything—I had doubted my ability.

A few weeks after I gave up my involvement in the music ministry, I met a group of devoted Catholics who deeply loved Christ and his Church. They were working to establish the format of an endeavor called, "The Good News Foundation." Through the generosity and inspiration of an elderly gentleman and his wife, this foundation had been established to evangelize, to bring the Good News of Jesus Christ to our local area. It surely was "Good News" to me!

Richard and I became involved, grateful for the fellowship of loving, Christian people, finding a place to use the gifts that God bestowed on us, and, once again, experiencing the blessings of Christian community.

The foundation invited expert teachers and ministers and brought them to share their expertise and giftedness with all of us. Because Richard and I believe that God brought us together and involved us in this foundation, we offered our home and hospitality to out-of-town speakers and presenters. We had

NOT MY WAY

three guest rooms waiting to be used. This small gesture of hospitality blessed us far more than our guests, for we met and shared God with many of his most gifted and talented disciples.

On one such occasion, a remarkable lady—Susan Blum—was coming to share her ministry of evangelization. She had been invited to teach an intensive two-day course on personal, one-to-one evangelization, sharing her years of experience in the field. She had been involved in the ministry of evangelization since 1979 and had written seven books on the topic of evangelization and spiritual renewal. Additionally, she presently served as the president and executive director of Isaiah Ministries, the largest band of Catholic clergy/lay mission preachers in the country.

When I knew Susan was coming to stay in our home, I read portions of one of her books, trying to get a feel for the house guest whom we would be entertaining. I loved her style of writing and looked forward to meeting her.

Reading Susan's autobiography, where she shared she had returned to school to complete a doctorate, reminded me once again of God's call to me to write. However, my inferiority fears and my lack of education convinced me once again that I couldn't! But I kept feeling an urgency from God to pray once again concerning writing.

When I met Susan, our hearts and spirits touched instantly. Here was a "soul mate," a "kindred spirit!" Meanwhile, since reading her book my call to write had intensified even more, almost with a sense of urgency. I didn't have a chance to share any of this with Susan that first night of her visit. Later I prayed, "Dearest Lord, please show me. What am I supposed to do?"

When Susan began her teaching the next morning at The Catholic Center, she spoke to about forty-five of us with the foundation. She said, "Many of you question your abilities and your giftedness. God wants to remind you that whatever he calls you to do, he enables. He will provide the gifts and ability to accomplish it! The gifts, the empowerment comes from him. If you feel that God is requiring something of you, *know* that he will help you do it. You don't need to look at the world's requirements. You don't need to be a Scripture scholar or a theologian, you don't need a college education to do what God calls you to do. All you need is a willing heart and a faith-filled 'Yes!' and he will help you do the rest."

NOT MY WAY

My ears heard the answer to my prayer and I was visibly touched. Susan noticed my tears and, when we broke for coffee, inquired as to what had happened. I shared that her words answered my prayer of the previous evening. Although time did not allow an explanation in greater detail, we agreed to speak later.

After her inspiring day of ministry and dinner with the foundation's Board of Directors that evening, the three of us, Richard, Susan and I, sat in my family room—our first opportunity for private time together and talked deep into the night. We shared our lives, finding many similar circumstances and experiences with God. I then shared with her my prayer of the night before about writing and my fears and inadequacies and explained how directly her teaching had spoken to me that morning.

Susan looked directly at me, "I travel extensively, Andrea, giving parish missions all over the country," she said, "and I hear many, many stories. You have a story to tell, which should be shared with others! You write it, and I'll edit and publish it!"

You are holding the fruit of that conversation in your hands right now! Unknown to me was the fact that Susan had established her own small publishing company just a year earlier!!!

Do we have an awesome God?
Does he answer prayer?
Is he loving and patient?
Does he know us personally and intimately?
Is it his desire to bless his children?
Will he give far more than we could ever hope or imagine?
Can he turn the circumstances of our lives from ruin to glory, from mourning into dancing?
Does he open the eyes of the blind? Set the captives free? Enable the weak? Heal the sick? Sustain the needy?
Did he bring me from my valley of humiliation to the high places in the kingdom of love?
With all my heart, I say "Yes!"
Are his ways my ways? "No! . . . They're much better!"

EPILOGUE

It is as if we are all walking on our road through life . . . our road to Emmaus . . . learning, experiencing, gathering information. We walk unaware of the Truth that accompanies us. Then, by some miracle, the eyes to our understanding are opened and we recognize Jesus. We tell it to those who are with us, who question and doubt and fear, until Jesus encounters them.

"Then he opened their minds to understand at last the many scriptures, reminding them that everything written about him by Moses and the prophets and in the psalms must all come true." Luke22:44

And it does, through him. Then, his promise of the Holy Spirit fills them with power, enabling them to tell others.

Over and over he fills us with his own Spirit, full enough to bring the Good News to others, but we leak. We begin empowered; then fear and doubt creep in and create cracks in our vessel and the power and the truth seep out leaving us unsure and empty, questioning our ability to effectively carry enough living water to quench anyone's thirst.

Over and over, mercifully and patiently, he waits . . . encouraging us . . . loving us . . . filling us . . . showing us *how* . . . telling us *when* and sometimes telling us *why*!

To be so full of ourselves inhibits the true filling with him. Thus, our testimony weakens, and our light flickers. It's hard to walk with sure feet on the Way when the light to our understanding dims and the one we serve cannot clearly be seen.

In love and compassion, we must help keep each other full, notice each others' cracks, and hold each other together with support and encouragement.

Then, when they say, "See how they love one another?" Jesus will be seen. Our testimony will speak. Our vessels will have accomplished the task for which they were created.

I pray with all my cracks and flaws that all the love and support I've received has enabled some to drink of the Living Water I carry.

NOT MY WAY

My love story is unending and continues because of the stubborn, unfailing, merciful love of the one who calls himself, "Love." I've learned and grown and become aware of real love, not the selfish, desperate, controlling need of another human being, but the selfless grace in acceptance, the honoring of another's will and decision, however difficult to comprehend.

I have learned to recognize and overcome the lie of worthlessness and unworthiness and accept the truth of my identity and integrity as God's child. I've learned to love God and his choices, to worship him, to go beyond bowing down to worship at the altar of my own desires, but to have faith in the the Way that is eternal, limitless, and unfathomable. I've become enlightened by the light to guide me through the dark terror of my ignorance and fear.

My family has grown, my life enriched. The joy promised by God has been received. Precious Richard and I are one with God as our center. Phyllis and Bill and Bob, my sister and brothers-in-law, are blessed additions to my life. Jolene and Rick—my new children—join Tom and Kathy, Dave and Wendy, along with all of our grandchildren. My Kelly, too, begins her new life with her Patrick.

My children and their children now are blessed to have three fathers who love them . . . Father God . . . gentle, precious Richard . . . and Tom, with his twinkling, Irish eyes, who remains totally cured of cancer after all these years.

I believe the sharing of my story, which clearly was *Not My Way* of doing things, will encourage others to leave their valley of humiliation and climb their mountain with the Good Shepherd, embrace his way, and live victorious lives.

"The Lord God is my strength, and he will make my feet like hinds' feet and he will make me to walk upon mine high places."
Habakkuk 3:19

INVITATION

Having spent many years devoted to proclaiming the Good News which is available to all, it is my fervent desire to equip everyone with the "Way" to embrace the "Truth" that set me free.

God assures and reassures all of us of his presence and availability. If we seek and ask, we will find.

God reveals his truth to us in Scripture. He tells us that he is our Father and he loves us, that our sin has separated us from him and we need a Savior. He sent Jesus, his son to gift us with eternal life if we believe in and accept him as the resurrected and living Christ (the anointed one, the Messiah). We need to believe in and receive Jesus as our personal Lord and Savior, recognize our sinfulness and repent (tell God we're sorry) and receive him into our hearts so our lives can be empowered and transformed.

I believe the first most difficult thing is to truly believe that we are loved unconditionally by God. The second is that we are really forgiven of our sins. I heard a story of God's love and mercy that helped me to believe:

One day while sitting next to a river, a man who had committed some dreadful sins was lamenting to himself about his terrible mistakes. "My guilt is so great and my pain overwhelming... what can I do?" he cried. He heard a voice speak clearly to him... "My child, gather in your mind all your terrible deeds and throw them into the river." He did what he was told and felt somewhat relieved but then the guilt of remembering them crept back into his mind and he again was overwhelmed. He heard the voice speak to him... "My child, your sins are forgiven. Go and sin no more, and my precious child, I have placed on the river bank a sign 'NO FISHIN!' Know that I have washed away your sins and with them my rememberance of them... When you are tempted to take upon yourself the weight of those sins, remember my sign and go in peace. I love you.

I have often remembered that story and marvel at the love, compassion, and mercy of God my Father.

NOT MY WAY

John 3 16: Yes, God so loved the world that he gave his only son, so that everyone who believes in him may not be lost but may have eternal life. (NJB)

Invitational Prayer

Dear Jesus, I acknowledge that I am a sinner. I am weak and I am sorry for and repent of all my sins. I desire to receive you into my heart as my Lord and Savior. Fill me with your spirit and grant me the gift of salvation so that I may live for all eternity with you. Amen.

NOT MY WAY

"THE REST OF THE STORY"... A NOTE FROM THE PUBLISHER

Not My Way would be incomplete unless I told you the "rest of the story." Andrea strongly believes that her entire life was orchestrated by a God who allowed particular events to happen, allowed special people to enter her life, and allowed her to make specific, definite choices as she struggled on the mountain trails... She's right! There are no coincidences... only "God incidences!"

My coming to Utica to present the evangelization seminar for the Good News Foundation was just such one of these, a "God-incidence!" Meeting Andrea couldn't possibly have been a mere coincidence since my visit was built upon such an intricate network of *other* events, *other* people, and *other* experiences *in my own life.* God had to have orchestrated it all ... over several years' time...up to the very last minute!

The week before I was scheduled to go, I became very ill. Flu-like symptoms turned into a terrible head cold and fever, eventually leading to laryngitis, tracheitis and bronchitis. Despite medical care and antibiotics, I did not recover as soon or as well as I had expected. In fact, I was getting worse! Finally, on the day before I was scheduled to leave, my doctor told me that I was on the verge of pneumonia and should cancel the trip.

I was so tempted to follow his advice, especially since I felt so awful, but I didn't know whether to follow my doctor's orders or not. What was God's will for me in this case? Like Andrea, I often demanded a physical manifestation of God's will for me. That evening I opened my Bible to the last chapter of Matthew's *Gospel.* I began to read Jesus' last recorded words before his Ascension, a very familiar passage, one upon which I based my entire life and ministry ... "Go ye therefore into the whole world and make disciples... Teach them everything I have commanded you, and know that I am with you always, even unto the end of time."

I had read this passage perhaps a hundred times before, maybe a thousand! The only word I saw on the page this time, though, was **"Go!!!"**

NOT MY WAY

So I went! And now you know the "rest of the story" ... definitely a "God incidence!"

It is not an accident or a coincidence, either, that you have chosen to read this account of God's presence in Andrea's life. I know that you will be blessed and inspired through it as I have been. Yes, as Andrea says, "Our God is an awesome God!"

Susan Blum Gerding, President
Jeremiah Press

PS—I wish you all could meet Andrea. She doesn't even realize how beautiful she is, inside and out! And Dundee truly is "Mr. Wonderful" ... oops, make that *"Dr. Wonderful!"* What a gift they both are!!!!